Berlitz®

Morocco

Cover: the Tin Mal Mosque in the Atlas

Right: Grand Mosque of Hassan II, Casablanca

TOP 10 ATTRACTIONS

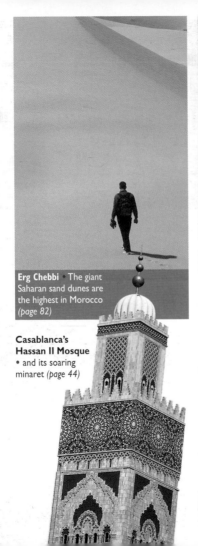

Fez • A World Heritage Site famed for its rich architecture *(page 56)*

Erg Chebbi • The giant Saharan sand dunes are the highest in Morocco *(page 82)*

Casablanca's Hassan II Mosque • and its soaring minaret *(page 44)*

Chaouen • This vestige of Moorish Andalusia was forgotten for 500 years *(page 34)*

Essaouira • A fortified fishing village on the Atlantic coast, whose strong on-shore winds have made it popular with windsurfers *(page 84)*

Rabat • The Hassan Tower minaret dominates the capital *(page 36)*

Volubilis • Its Roman villas and mosaics are remarkably well preserved *(page 52)*

The Berber villages of the High Atlas • Extraordinary places that seem to be part of the landscape *(page 76)*

Meknes • The Imperial capital under Sultan Moulay Ismail *(page 46)*

The souks of Marrakesh • From spices to leather to fine ceramics and furnishings – it's all here *(page 69)*

CONTENTS

89

62

48

Features

71

64

93

INTRODUCTION

Morocco is one of the world's most exotic destinations, yet it lies right at Europe's doorstep, a mere 14km (9 miles) south of Spain. It is a country of extravagant architecture and labyrinthine walled cities; of markets filled with dazzling tribal crafts and works of delicate beauty; of windsurfers on the wild beaches of the Atlantic coast; and hikers amid the almond blossom and waterfalls of the snow-capped High Atlas Mountains.

Everywhere the pageant of life in Morocco is accompanied by music – pounding African rhythms heard in the souks of the south, or the classical Andalusian music of Meknes, Tetouan and Fez in the north that echoes the intricate, 1,000-year-old traditions of Moorish Spain. Dine by candlelight in former palaces while being serenaded by soft, trance-like Gnaoua music (brought to Morocco from West Africa centuries ago); walk through one of the exquisite gardens in Marrakesh before twilight and you'll find them filled with birdsong.

Inspiring landscape
The glorious Moroccan countryside and its exceptional quality of light have seduced famous painters including Delacroix, Dufy and Matisse.

Morocco is often breathtakingly beautiful. The idyllic and isolated Berber villages of the High Atlas seem untouched by time (except for the satellite dishes). In sophisticated cities like Fez, Essaouira and Marrakesh the medieval intricacies of their medinas go hand in hand with fashionable roof-top bars and chic renovated *riads* (a traditional Moroccan house with a courtyard; *see page 73*).

The dramatic fortified village of Aït Benhaddou

Situated at the northwestern corner of the African continent, Morocco faces Europe across the narrow Strait of Gibraltar. It stretches for roughly 2,000km (1,240 miles) from the Mediterranean coast at Tangier to the sands of the Sahara. The country is dominated by the High and Middle Atlas Mountains, a series of parallel ranges that run southwest from the Algerian border to the Atlantic coast, isolating the coastal plain from the rest of Africa.

Contrasting Landscapes

The landscapes of Morocco are extremely varied. The jagged limestone peaks of the Rif Mountains to the southeast of Tangier give way to the cultivated coastal plains between Rabat and Casablanca and the foothills of the Atlas Mountains. The dramatic High Atlas range extends for 700km (430 miles) in a series of long ridges reaching 4,167m (13,670ft) at Mount Toubkal, the highest point in North Africa. South of the Atlas runs the Anti Atlas range, with its spectacular rock formations, straight through the lush Souss Valley. Further south the landscape becomes dry and desolate, as befits the fringes of the Sahara Desert, but enlivened by fertile river valleys, with pockets of terrace farming, and green splashes of date palm oases.

Colourful street life
in Marrakesh

Climate

As with the landscape, so with the climate. The coast from Tangier to Agadir has a temperate climate, averaging 15°C (60°F) in winter and 25°C (75°F) in summer; rainfall is concentrated in the north, and falls mainly in winter; the southern beach resort of Agadir can have as many as 300 days of sunshine a year. The inland cities of Fez, Meknes and Marrakesh are slightly cooler in winter and brutally hot in summer, but the most extreme variations occur in the mountains. On the summit ridges of the Atlas, temperatures plummet to -20°C (-8°F) in midwinter, and soar to 40°C (105°F) during the summer when the desert winds blow in from the east.

A Mosaic of Cultures

Today there are some 33 million Moroccans, descendants of aboriginal Berbers as well as of the Arabs who invaded the region in the 7th century. Although in many parts of the country these two peoples have blended together and have much in common, there are still pure Berbers in the more remote mountain areas. Many Berbers have paler skin, reddish or brown hair, and green or blue eyes. There are three different Berber dialects in Morocco: Tarfit in the Rif (1.5 million speakers), Tamazight in the High Atlas (3 million) and Tashalit in the Souss Valley region (3–4 million). Berber schools are allowed to teach in Berber rather than Arabic.

Added to this mix are the descendants of hundreds of thousands of Muslims and Jews who fled to Morocco from El Andalus (Andalusia) in southern Spain at the time of the Christian reconquest during the 14th and 15th centuries; and the descendants of black African slaves imported from West Africa during the Saadi dynasty. In the far south of the country you will also meet the Tuareg, nomadic tribesmen of the

Mint Tea

No visit to a Moroccan home would be complete without the ritual of mint tea, or *thé à la menthe*, indisputably Morocco's national drink. Prepared in a *bulbous*, or squat, curved teapot made of silver, pewter or enamel, the tea is often served in little coloured glasses. Delicious, refreshing and highly sweetened, it is made from an infusion of green tea with sprigs of fresh mint. Occasionally pine kernels or orange flowers may be added. To pour the tea, the teapot is held very high above the glass in order to aerate the liquid as it falls.

Mint tea is served throughout the day and after meals (it is said to aid digestion). Traders in the souks (markets) are likely to offer you a glass or two after concluding a successful bargain.

Sahara, often identified by their darker skins and blue robes.

This huge and varied country is unified by Islam, the national religion, of which the leader is King Mohammed VI, who commands great respect. Morocco is a progressive Muslim state, notably on the issue of women's rights.

Moroccan Hospitality

Moroccans, whether Arab or Berber, always offer a warm welcome to visitors, and their famous hospitality – a characteristic that has risen up from the isolated desert outposts of the Sa-

Try some *tajine*!

hara – extends especially to foreign visitors. Wherever you are in Morocco, you will regularly be offered a glass or two of mint tea *(see box opposite)*, a long-established custom and sign of friendship, and you may even receive an invitation to dine at the family home. Don't feel obliged to take people up on their offers of dinner, however – if such a thing doesn't appeal, a polite excuse will suffice, and offers of this kind should not be viewed with suspicion. The hustlers you may come across in the tourist areas are unrepresentative of the people as a whole.

If you have the chance to get off the beaten track and stay in a Berber village in the mountains, the experience will linger in your memory long after you return home.

A BRIEF HISTORY

Morocco is a vast and varied territory that was only relatively recently united into a modern nation state. Its long history records a struggle for ascendancy between the Berber tribes of the mountains and the Arabs of the plains, the rise and fall of powerful dynasties, the creation and collapse of mighty empires, and, from the 18th century, manipulation and exploitation by European powers seeking to expand their empires.

The First Settlers

The ancient Greeks called this land the country of Atlas, after the Titan who was condemned by Zeus to bear the heavens upon his shoulders. Here, at the western extremity of their world, where the chariot of the sun god Helios vanished over the horizon each night and the Hesperides, or Daughters of Evening, tended their magical garden, Atlas watched over his huge herds of sheep and cattle. According to a later legend, the hero Perseus showed him the head of the Gorgon Medusa to punish him for refusing to give him shelter, and Atlas was turned into the mountain range that still bears his name.

Berber women's festive costume has not changed for centuries

The Phoenicians were the first to explore this far western land, setting up a trading post at Liks (Lixus) on the Moroccan coast around 1000BC. In the succeeding centuries they and their descendants, the Carthaginians (whose home city was near modern Tunis), founded outposts at Tangier and Essaouira, while also building a town on the site of present-day Rabat. Greek traders called the fierce inhabitants of the interior *barbaroi*, meaning 'not of our people', a name that has persisted through the ages as 'Berber' (the English word 'barbarian' has the same root).

The origins of the Berbers remain a mystery. Some theories link them with the Celts, the Basques, and even the tribes

of Canaan (northern Lebanon), but it's far more likely that they are descendants of the Neolithic Capsian culture, which spread through North Africa during the 5th and 6th millennia BC. Berbers (or Amaziah) have preserved their own languages and traditional customs to the present day.

Throughout the 3rd and 4th centuries BC, Berber kingdoms were established in many parts of Morocco. From these small strongholds, over the course of the next thousand years, the Berber people were to build mighty empires that ruled all of North Africa and most of Spain. First, however, came the Romans.

Roman Morocco

After the ancient city of Carthage (near modern Tunis) fell to Rome in 146BC, the North African coast to the west was added to the Roman Empire as the provinces of Numidia

Volubilis, Morocco's most extensive Roman remains

(which roughly corresponds to modern Algeria) and Mauritania (modern Morocco). From 25BC to AD23 Mauritania was ruled by Juba II, a handsome young Berber king installed by the Emperor Augustus. A fine scholar, Juba was educated in Rome and made journeys to countries in distant parts of Arabia to gather material for the many books he wrote. His wife, Cleopatra Selene, was the daughter of Mark Antony and Cleopatra. A fine bronze statue of Juba II, found at the site of Volubilis, which may have served as Juba's capital, is on display at the Archaeological Museum in Rabat.

The Romans developed the city of Sala Colonia (modern Chellah) on the site of present-day Rabat. The Roman Empire made few deep inroads into Morocco, so the language and culture of the mountain Berbers were little affected by Roman civilisation. Carthaginian refugees probably fled to this region at the fringe of Roman control.

The Muslim Conquest

The 7th century saw the rise of Islam in Arabia. In the early years believers were organised into a small, close-knit community headed by the Prophet Mohammed himself. Within a century of Mohammed's death in AD632, Muslim armies had conquered the whole of the Middle East, including Persia (Iran), all of North Africa and parts of Spain and France.

In 670 the Arab general Oqba ibn Nafi founded the holy city of Kairouan in Tunisia. From Kairouan, in 682, Oqba led his raiding armies all the way to the Atlantic coast of Morocco. He named the land *al Maghrib al-Aksa*, Arabic for 'the furthest west'. This remains Morocco's name in Arabic to this day.

The prospect of an invasion of the rich Spanish peninsula made many Berbers convert to Islam and join the Muslim armies to carry the banner of Islam across the Mediterranean.

For the next six centuries, the Islamic civilisation of Spain and Morocco outshone anything in Christian Europe.

From the time of the Muslim Conquest to the formation of a Protectorate in the 20th century, the political history of Morocco is that of an uninterrupted succession of dynasties. After consolidating power, subduing enemies, and building monumental cities, mosques and palaces, each successive regime slid into decadence, leading to weak government, political chaos and bitter fighting, until a new faction stepped in to fill the power vacuum.

The Idrissids

Moulay Idriss, a descendant of the Prophet Mohammed, arrived in Volubilis in 788 and was proclaimed king by the chief of the local Berber tribes. As a descendant of the Prophet, he possessed great *baraka* ('divine blessing'), which was believed to bring good fortune to his followers. As a result his power and influence grew rapidly.

Alarmed by the growing influence of Idriss, Harun al-Rashid, the powerful Caliph of Baghdad, dispatched an assassin with a vial of poison to murder his distant rival. Moulay Idriss was buried near the city of Volubilis, and the village that contains his tomb (and still bears his name) is one of the most sacred shrines in Morocco.

His son, Moulay Idriss II, founded an impressive capital for the Idrissid Empire at Fez, not far from the Roman city of Volubilis. His city was built around the area that is now occupied by the great Kairaouine Mosque. Its population increased significantly with the influx of refugees fleeing from political upheavals in the great Islamic cities of Kairouan in Tunisia and Córdoba in Spain. Idriss II died in 828, and his empire was split among his eight sons. This led to a weakening of the state and paved the way for a new regime characterised by strict religious practice.

Detail of the mausoleum of Moulay Idriss II, founder of Fez

The Almoravids

The next Moroccan dynasty had its origins among the Berber tribes of the desert. A young Muslim religious student named Abdallah ibn Yasin moved south from the region of Agadir to preach to the Berbers and soon emerged as a spirited and vigorous leader. His teachings were based on the strictest discipline: missing prayers was punished with a whipping. Even the Berbers, used to the hardships of life in the Sahara, found Ibn Yasin's regime too harsh, and he and his band of followers were pushed south across the desert. There they built a fortified monastery (in Arabic, a *ribat*) on the sub-Saharan coast in Mauritania, and created a community of religious warriors similar to the Christian Knights of the Crusades.

Between 1054 and 1059 a small army of these puritans swept northwards and conquered southern Morocco, wrecking drinking places, smashing up musical instruments and imposing their strict religious code. In 1056 they took

Taroudannt, and in 1062 founded their capital, Marrakesh. They captured Fez in 1069.

In 1086 the dynasty received a plea for help from the Muslim kingdoms of Spain, who were under attack from Christian armies. The Almoravids, led by Yusuf ibn Tashfin, flooded into Spain and quickly took control in Córdoba, Granada and Seville. Tashfin soon became the most powerful Muslim ruler in Spain and the Maghreb (the Arabic name for the whole of north-west Africa). Tashfin's son Ali ben Youssef ruled the empire from 1107 to 1143, and in his time the fierce, austere Almoravids adopted the habits of dissolute but highly cultured Muslim Andalusia. Despite their violent fanaticism, they initiated a golden age of Moroccan art and culture. The richness of Hispano-Islamic art and architecture

Morocco's Jewish Community

The 2,000-year-old Jewish community in Morocco has contributed to the nation's cultural mosaic despite its small size (270,000 in 1950). The first Jews in Morocco were refugees from the Judean rebellions against Rome in AD70 and 135. Others descended from Berber tribes converted to Judaism in the centuries before the rise of Islam, or from Spanish Jews exiled by the edicts of the Catholic Monarchs Ferdinand and Isabella in 1492.

Until the early 20th century, Moroccan Jews were required to live in *mellahs*, quarters reserved for them in every major city, where their activities were restricted but also protected. They developed high levels of professional skills, notably in medicine and silversmithing.

During World War II the Moroccan Jews escaped the Holocaust because King Mohammed V refused to deport them. After 1956, the majority of them emigrated to Israel and France. The Moroccan government permits them, as well as their descendants, to return to Morocco, on holiday or for business. The present Jewish community numbers around 6,000, most of them elderly, and is concentrated in Casablanca.

spread throughout Morocco, especially in Marrakesh, the new capital. Fez, the former capital city, was graced with the splendid Kairaouine Mosque.

The Almohads

The start of the 12th century saw the emergence of another radical religious reformer. Ibn Tumert, a Moroccan theological student and holy man, travelled east to visit the prestigious Muslim colleges of the Arabian heartland. Fired with religious fervour, he returned to Morocco to preach a unitarian doctrine and soon founded a new puritanical sect, the Almohads or 'Unitarians'.

Almohad architecture: the Kasbah Mosque, Marrakesh

They, too, banned all luxuries, including the playing of musical instruments.

A religious fanatic, Ibn Tumert was unpopular with local officials, but he acquired a large following of zealots. Together they imitated the example of the earlier Almoravids and withdrew to a fortress-monastery at Tin Mal, in the High Atlas mountains between Marrakesh and Taroudannt.

Ibn Tumert died in 1130 but his right-hand man, Abd el Moumen, carried on the crusade. Abd el Moumen was more warrior than preacher, however, and he proved to be an outstanding general. In two campaigns between 1151 and 1159 he displaced the Almoravids and seized control of the whole of North Africa, eventually taking over all of Muslim Spain. The Almohad empire lasted for more than a century, and during the reign of Yacoub el Mansour ('the Conqueror', grandson of Abd el Moumen), it brought Moroccan power and civilisation to a peak. The territory under Almohad rule extended from Morocco to Algeria, Tunisia and part of Libya, as well as deep into Spain. The Moorish culture of Andalusia seduced the Almohads just as it had the Almoravids. In their most glorious period (1160–1210) they created some of the most beautiful monuments of Islamic art. The influence of Spanish Muslim art can be found in the masterpieces of Almohad architecture in Morocco – the Koutoubia Minaret in Marrakesh, for example, and the Hassan Tower and Oudaia Kasbah Gate in Rabat. Eventually, the power of the Almohad rulers weakened and anarchy reigned in Marrakesh, as various warring clans battled for control of territory.

The Tin Mal Mosque, seat of the Almohad dynasty

The Merinids

Another Berber tribe, the Beni Merin, seized power in Fez in 1248 and established the Merinid dynasty. They were motivated not by religious fanaticism but by greed for land, power and riches. By the time they took Marrakesh in 1269, the whole country had fallen under their sway. Abou Hassan, known as the Black Sultan, reorganised the empire from the Atlantic coast to the Gulf of Gabes in Tunisia and ruled it with an iron hand for 30 years.

Although their political achievements could not be compared with those of the Almohads, the Merinids left a substantial cultural legacy. A hundred years of Merinid rule brought glory to Fez, just as Almohad rule had to Marrakesh. To embellish their imperial capital, the Merinids constructed the 'new' city of Fez el Jdid, and built the two most exquisite *medersas* (religious colleges) in the old city, the El Attarine (1325) and the Bou Inania (1355). The tombs of the Merinid kings, in ruins today, still dominate Fez from a nearby hill. In Rabat, the massive Chellah was the Merinids' fortified cemetery, and the magnificent Alhambra Palace in Granada, Spain, was built during their reign.

The demise of the Merinids in the 15th century marked the end of Berber domination in Morocco.

Christian Encroachments

In the early 15th century piracy became a way of attacking Christians, and it provided an excuse for the latter to intervene in Morocco. Spain, after centuries of Muslim domination, was especially motivated by revenge, and both Spain and Portugal sent warships and armies after the Muslim and Jewish refugees who had fled to Morocco to escape the Spanish Inquisition. By the early 1500s, Portugal held most of the important towns along the Atlantic coast of Morocco; a few decades later the Spaniards took over Sebta (Ceuta).

The Three Kings

The Battle of the Three Kings involved Portugal's Sebastian I, his ally the deposed Sultan Mohammed el Mutawakkil, and the Saadian Sultan Abd el Malik, the victor. All three died in the battle.

The Saadians

The Saadi dynasty, a clan of Arab origin descended from the Prophet Mohammed, surged north from their homeland in the Draa Valley to confront the Christian invaders. They took Agadir from the Portuguese in 1541, and by 1576 had installed themselves in Fez as the new rulers of Morocco. In 1578 they defeated the Portuguese in the Battle of the Three Kings and extended their empire south to Timbuktu in Mali, where they traded in gold, sugar and slaves. Marrakesh was the Saadians' favoured city, and under Sultan Ahmed el Mansour (1578–1603), the greatest of the 11 Saadian sultans, they lavished enormous wealth on such monuments as the palace of El Badi and the exquisite Saadian Tombs. Following the death of Sultan Ahmed in 1603, the dynasty fragmented and the great age of medieval Moroccan independence was over.

The Alaouites

A new national leadership emerged with the Alaouite dynasty, who originated from the oases of the Tafilalet, on the edge of the Sahara desert south of Erfoud. They were invited by the people of Fez to bring order to the country. By 1672 the Alaouites had control of Marrakesh, and the brutal but effective sultan Moulay Ismail (ruled 1672–1727) had come to power. Moulay Ismail was a man with powerful appetites (it is said he fathered more than 1,000 children) and a thirst for glory. A cruel and ruthless tyrant, Ismail nevertheless succeeded in uniting much of the country and bringing it to the attention of Europe. Forsaking the traditional imperial cities of Marrakesh and Fez, he built his own imperial city at Meknes, where he entertained foreign ambassadors in palatial luxury that rivalled that of Versailles.

After the death of Moulay Ismail, Morocco again slumped into decades of anarchy and privation. His numerous sons and the *abids* (soldiers descended from African slaves) disputed the throne for 30 years. By contrast, the sultan Mohammed ibn Abdullah, who built Essaouira, was a pious and peace-loving man. He was succeeded by his sons. Other capable Alaouite monarchs came to the throne in the late 18th century but, by that time, Europe was starting to colonise Africa, a threat emphasised by the French seizure of Algiers in 1830.

The Franco-Spanish Protectorate

Moulay Abdullah Abderrahman, Alaouite sultan from 1822–59

Throughout the 19th century resourceful Alaouite sultans successfully played one European power against another. Yet Morocco became increasingly dependent on French military protection, and the Treaty of Fez in 1912 made it into a Franco-Spanish Protectorate, with its capital in Rabat. The French, under the administration of Marshal Lyautey, governed the central and southern parts of the country. Spain controlled the northernmost portion with the exception of Tangier, which became an International Zone.

The Protectorate did bring some of the hallmarks of the Western world to Moroccan life: roads and railways were built, a modern education system was established, and *villes nouvelles* (new towns) were laid out alongside the old medinas (the old Arab quarters). Agriculture and mining were also encouraged. These were turbulent years, however, and for the young Moroccans growing up in the 1920s, progress was worthless without independence. The young crown prince Mohammed V of the Alaouite dynasty, who in 1927 was chosen by the French as sultan, sympathised in silence with the movement for independence, but was in no position to act.

Independence

France's hold on Morocco was weakened during World War II, and Moroccan nationalists came out in the open to form the Istiqlal (Independence) Party. Mohammed V was firmly

The national flag at the royal palace, Rabat

on their side. After World War II, in a vain attempt to suppress Moroccan nationalism, the French exiled Mohammed V and his family to Corsica and then Madagascar. The plan backfired because it made the sultan a popular symbol of courage and resistance to foreign rule. By 1955 the French were forced to recall Mohammed V from exile. He returned a hero; in March 1956, independence was granted and Morocco was once again united under the independent rule of an Alaouite king.

Mass rally

Some 350,000 unarmed Moroccan civilians were mobilised for the Green March. On 6 November 1975 they marched south across the frontier waving flags and copies of the Koran.

Mohammed V had just embarked upon his ambitious plans for progress and development when he died in 1961, after a minor operation. The nation was shocked at the untimely passing of the greatest Alaouite sovereign since Moulay Ismail. He retains a special place in the hearts of Moroccans, who regularly come to pay their respects at his mausoleum in Rabat. Today the main street in every town in the country is named after him.

Mohammed V's son ascended the throne as King Hassan II and introduced a new constitution, declaring Morocco to be a 'social, democratic and constitutional monarchy'. As a result, parliamentary elections are held every six years, but power remains largely in the hands of the king. As a *sharif*, the king is also Commander of the Faithful, Morocco's religious leader.

The Green March

One of the most important events of King Hassan's reign was the *Marche Verte* (Green March) of November 1975, when he led 350,000 unarmed civilians into the former Spanish colony of Western Sahara to assert Moroccan sovereignty over the region. The occupation was resisted by the guerrillas of the Popular Front for the Liberation of Saguia el Hamra and Rio de Oro (better known as the Polisario), but by 1987 Hassan had succeeded in controlling the rebels with a remarkable 2,000-km- (1,250-mile-) long defensive sand wall around the new territory. A peace plan drafted by the United Nations proposed a ceasefire, to be followed by a referendum, under international control, to give the people of the thinly populated area the choice between independence or remaining part of Morocco. However, after all these years sovereignty over the Western Sahara has still to be determined. The long-promised referendum among the people has yet to take place.

Progressive Policies

Although the late King Hassan maintained Morocco's age-old traditions during his 38-year reign, he also promoted progressive policies in the fields of health, education and economics. His son Mohammed VI, who succeeded to the throne immediately on his father's death in 1999, has continued and developed these and related reforms; and in 2000 the UN launched the Arab world's first centre for human rights training and information in Rabat.

Mohammed VI succeeded to the throne in 1999

Morocco is busy building, expanding and modernising (the population has doubled in the past 30 years), but its remarkable culture and way of life endure and continue to fascinate and beguile legions of visitors.

Historical Landmarks

c. 1000BC Phoenician sailors build trading posts along the coast.

146 BC Carthage falls to Rome. Northern Morocco included in province of Mauritania.

AD 3rd–4th century Roman Empire withdraws from Morocco.

682 Muslim conquest under Oqba ibn Nafi.

711 The Moors launch their conquest of Spain.

788–926 Idrissid dynasty: Moulay Idriss II founds Fez.

1054–1143 Almoravid dynasty: Marrakesh founded in 1102 by Yusuf ibn Tashfin.

Early 12th century–1248 Almohad dynasty. Their empire includes Morocco, Algeria, Tunisia, Libya and Spain.

1248–1465 Merinid dynasty: the last Berber dynasty.

15th century Anarchy reigns. In Spain, the Catholic Monarchs Ferdinand and Isabella complete the Reconquista from the Moors: Granada, the last Moorish bastion, falls in 1492.

Mid-16th–mid-17th centuries Saadian dynasty establish their capital at Marrakesh. Portuguese defeated at Battle of Three Kings in 1578. Empire extends to Mali.

1666–present Alaouite dynasty ushers in national revival.

1672 Moulay Ismail builds his Imperial City located at Meknes.

18th–19th centuries Progressive colonisation of Africa and increasing European interference in Morocco's affairs.

1912 Franco-Spanish Protectorate established. Tangier becomes an International Zone

1956 Morocco granted independence.

1961 King Hassan II ascends to the throne.

1975 'Green March' into the Spanish Sahara.

1999 King Hassan II dies. His son, Mohammed VI, succeeds to the throne.

2003 Suicide bombings in Casablanca kill 41 people.

2004 Huge earthquake hits the north, killing over 500 people.

2005–6 Demonstrations and riots backed by the Polisario Front occur in Laayoune in support of independence for Western Sahara.

WHERE TO GO

Intricate medinas, unspoiled natural beauty, mysterious desert kasbahs, and endlessly fascinating souks – Morocco needs to be enjoyed at a slow pace, with ample time to investigate and wander. It would be impossible to see all that the country has to offer in a single trip, so it pays to be selective *(for highlights, see pages 2–3)*. Topping the list for most first-time visitors are the four magnificent Imperial Cities – Fez, Meknes, Rabat and Marrakesh. It's in these cities that the splendour of past Moroccan empires is concentrated. The independent traveller can reach them all by train or bus, but if you plan to explore south of Marrakesh, a hire car is useful *(see page 109)*.

The most northern point of arrival, and the port of entry for people taking the ferry from Spain or Gibraltar, is Tangier.

TANGIER (TANGER)

Located at the northern tip of Morocco, where Africa and Europe face each other across the Strait of Gibraltar, Tangier has always held a special position in Moroccan history. The Phoenicians set up a trading post here, and later the Romans founded the town of Tingis. Succeeding centuries saw Tangier fall under Vandal, Byzantine, Arab, Moroccan, Spanish and Portuguese rule; for a brief period (1662–84) it even belonged to England, as part of the dowry of the Portuguese Catherine of Braganza, the bride of Charles II. Under British rule, extensive fortifications were erected.

After the Franco-Spanish Protectorate was established in 1912 the city was granted special status as an International

Shade by a mosque in the kasbah of Tangier

Spices in the souk

Zone. It was governed by a commission of foreign diplomats, and this arrangement, together with the city's special privileges as a free port, attracted many European and American expatriates and adventurers. Although Tangier is as much a part of Morocco as Rabat or Marrakesh, it retains a cosmopolitan flavour quite distinct from the rest of the country. Its *souk* is somewhat touristy, but the *medina* (old Arab quarter) offers some real treasures.

During the Protectorate northern Morocco was governed by Spain, and Spanish tends to be more widely spoken than French in Tangier and the surrounding region.

The Ville Nouvelle

Like all Moroccan cities, Tangier consists of a walled medina, or old town, as well as a modern quarter built during the Protectorate, called the *Ville Nouvelle* (new town). At the centre of the Ville Nouvelle is the **Place de France** and the tree-lined **Boulevard Pasteur**, with its busy cafés and crowded restaurants, banks and travel agencies. A terrace at the end of Boulevard Pasteur has a fine view of the harbour and the Spanish mainland; in the evenings it is a favourite meeting-place for tourists and locals alike.

Rue de la Liberté (Zankat el Houria), the site of the elegant El Minzah Hotel *(see page 135)*, leads down to the old marketplace of the **Grand Socco**. Just off it, on Rue de l'Angleterre, is a large white villa, formerly the British Consulate, which houses the **Museum of Contemporary Art of the City of Tangier** (open Tues–Sun 9am–12.30pm and 3–6pm), with an interesting collection of works by contemporary Moroccan painters.

Easily accessible from Rue du Portugal is the **Old American Legation**, a building given to the Americans by Sultan Moulay Slimane, whose government was the first in the world to recognise American independence in 1776. It now houses a small museum on the city's history (open Mon–Fri 10am–1pm and 3–5pm or by appointment, tel: 039 93 53 17). The Grand Socco is the terminus for city buses and has a large taxi rank. There are city beaches, but those outside the town, accessible by car or taxi, are cleaner and quieter.

The Medina

Tangier's medina is a maze of narrow streets on the hillside above the harbour. **Rue es-Siaghin** (or Silversmiths' Street) leads downhill from the Grand Socco to the Petit Socco; side

Matisse in Tangier

The painter and sculptor Henri Matisse (1869–1954) lived in Tangier from the end of January to mid-April 1912, and from October 1912 to mid-February 1913. These two brief periods had a lasting influence on his work. Lured to Tangier by the special quality of the light, he initially had to brave several weeks of rain. Yet he completed 23 paintings and some 60 drawings. Obliged to work indoors, he painted the still life *The Vase of Iris* (February 1912). The bad weather also explains the luxuriant vegetation in *Park in Tangier*, painted at the end of his first stay.

Other works from his time in Tangier are portraits of men, painted with a few strokes of colour, and three paintings of the young Jewess Zorah. There is little doubt that the intense blue that characterises Matisse's later works was inspired by the sea at Tangier.

Writers' retreat

Tangier played host to Cecil Beaton, Tennessee Williams and William Burroughs, who gained inspiration for episodes in *The Naked Lunch* in the Petit Socco.

streets to the right are filled with shops. The 17th-century **kasbah,** or fortified precinct, occupies the highest point in the medina, perched on a cliff-top above the sea. Here Sultan Moulay Ismail had built **Dar el Makhzen**, a palace that today houses the **Museum of Moroccan Arts and Antiquities** (open Wed–Mon 9am–1pm and 3–6pm), with treasures such as illuminated Korans, fine textiles, wood and metal work, Berber carpets, jewellery and ceramics.

At the entrance to the main part of the palace is the former treasury, the **Bit el Mal**. Rooms overlooking the *méchouar* (courtyard) house the sultan's gigantic cedarwood strongboxes that were once filled with gold and gems. Cross the *méchouar* to the observation point for a spectacular view across the strait to Gibraltar and Spain.

A 15-minute walk west of the kasbah, along the coast, brings you to **Palais Mendoub**, former Tangier home of the late American billionaire Malcolm Forbes. This large white villa once contained a museum of military miniatures, which were a passion of Forbes. It was here that he held his $2-million 70th birthday bash, an event that recalled the extravagant parties given by Barbara Hutton in Tangier.

Five minutes further west along the coast is the delightful **Café Hafa** (open during daylight hours). Perched halfway down a cliff with marvellous views out to sea, for decades it has been a meeting place for Tangier's literary intelligensia and expatriate community.

Another popular place for tea is the terrace of the old **Hotel Continental** overlooking the port; the cavernous, Moroccan crafts bazaar inside the hotel has a large selection of goods at reasonable prices.

Excursions from Tangier

Along the road to Rabat, 40km (26 miles) south of Tangier, lies the charming town of **Asilah**. Just off the main coastal road, Asilah is a white-walled Atlantic fishing port, complete with an impressive kasbah. In August the town hosts an international arts festival, a highlight of the cultural year.

Asilah was captured in 1471 by the Portuguese, who built the impressive walls and bastions enclosing the medina. Spanish occupation followed, and it was not until the end of the 17th century that Sultan Moulay Ismail recaptured the town for Morocco. At the start of the 20th century, Asilah was the stronghold of Raissouli, a brigand notorious for kidnapping foreigners and holding them for ransom. At the height of his power, Raissouli built a palace within the kasbah walls, overlooking the sea. He is said to have forced criminals to fling themselves from the top windows on to

The white-walled fishing port of Asilah, on the Atlantic coast

the rocks 30 metres (100ft) below. The palace is open during the yearly festival and is occasionally used as an exhibition space.

The medina of Asilah is delightful and easy to explore independently. Enter at **Bab el Kasaba** in the medina's northern wall and continue on the straight road past the great mosque and government offices; then turn right, cross the large square and continue right to the small main street of surprisingly good craft and antiquities shops. Colourful painted murals adorn the walls of a number of houses; the parapet at the southeastern tip of the medina overlooks the sea and provides wonderful vistas of the town.

Just outside Bab el Kasaba, **Casa Garcia** *(see page 138)* heads the list of pleasant restaurants serving fresh seafood. North of the harbour, and the construction site of a new marina, Asilah's splendid beach stretches for miles.

Another 38km (24 miles) south of Asilah lie the ruins of ancient **Lixus** (open site, no admission charge, closed in winter). The first settlement to be built here, a Phoenician trading post, may have been established as early as the 11th century BC. Lixus was an important centre for the Roman province of Mauretania Tingitana, and it grew rich shipping salt and fish to the capital city of Tingis (Tangier). What is left of the fish-salting factories are down by the main road. The remains of several temples, baths and a theatre are scattered over the top of the hill.

High in the Rif Mountains 120km (75 miles) from Tangier, **Chaouen** (sometimes spelled Chefchaouen) was founded in 1471 by Moulay Rashid, a follower of Moulay Abdesalam ben Mchich, the patron saint of the Djebali tribesman, whose sacred tomb near Chaouen had already been attracting pilgrims for centuries. In the following decades, Muslims and Jewish refugees arrived who were fleeing the Christian reconquest of Spain. The remote mountain

Chaouen, in the heart of the Rif countryside

stronghold became increasingly anti-European and autonomous. Until the Spanish arrived in 1920, only two Europeans (in disguise) succeeded in reaching it and leaving undetected. The Spanish also discovered a community of Jews descended from refugee settlers who still spoke medieval Castilian. Although it attracts many tourists, this 500-year-old piece of Moorish Andalusia hidden in the Rif countryside still possesses an air of mystery, and remains one of Morocco's prettiest towns.

The main square in the medina, **Place Outa el Hammam**, is lined with cafés. On one side is the beautiful kasbah, its walls enclosing a small museum and tranquil garden. In keeping with the town's otherworldliness, the pre-dawn call to prayer in Chaouen is a soft choir of voices that echoes in the surrounding mountains. Information on hikes as well as easy walks in the area, with or without guides, is available from Chaouen's many hotels and simple *pensions*.

RABAT

The capital city of modern Morocco lies at the mouth of the Bou Regreg river. The site was probably occupied by Phoenicians as early as the 11th century BC, and the Romans built their southernmost port, Sala Colonia, here in the 1st century AD. But it was not until the 10th century that a local Berber tribe founded the city of Salé on the right bank of the river mouth, and built a *ribat* (fortified camp) on a bluff at the western extremity of the estuary's south bank.

During the 12th century, **Rabat** became the imperial capital of the great Almohad conqueror Yacoub el Mansour, who ruled over an area that stretched from Tunisia to northern Spain. After his death Rabat lost much of its importance, and it was the cities of Fez, Meknes and Marrakesh that prospered in the centuries that followed.

Rabat did not recover its status as capital until the establishment of the Franco-Spanish Protectorate in 1912, when Marshal Lyautey made it the administrative capital; and it was only when Morocco regained its full independence in 1956 that the city became capital of the new kingdom.

Today Rabat and its sister town of Salé form a conurbation of almost 1.6 million people. Rabat, with its gracious architecture, leafy boulevards and cafés has a relaxed, almost genteel atmosphere. **Avenue Mohammed V**, the principal artery, cuts a broad, sunny swathe through the new town, past government buildings, banks, the railway station and the main post office. Pedestrians stroll in the shady shopping arcades on either side, stopping at the busy cafés to enjoy a coffee or mint tea.

A divided city

Only the river separates Rabat from its twin, the former pirate base of Salé. Yet the ambiance in each town could hardly be more different.

Entrance to the Royal Palace in Rabat, Morocco's capital

The Medina

If you follow Avenue Mohammed V north (turn left coming out of the railway station), you will eventually reach the entrance to Rabat's medina. Pass through the 17th-century Andalusian wall – note the tidy municipal market on the left – and then turn right into Rue es Souika. Although some of the shops along this street sell leather and copper items unquestionably aimed at the tourist trade, most of them cater to local needs. As the minaret of the **Grand Mosque** comes into view on the right, the street enters the roofed-over **Souk es Sebat**, which is filled with a variety of shops selling practical items and foodstuffs. Where the Souk es Sebat emerges into the daylight, turn left into **Rue des Consuls**, the only street in which foreign consuls could formerly set up shop. Today it is largely, but not exclusively, a tourist shopping street, with merchants selling carpets and rugs, jewellery and antiques as well as kaftans, *jellabas* and leather goods.

The Crafts Museum in the Oudaia Kasbah

At the end of Rue des Consuls you'll see the massive walls of the **Oudaia Kasbah**. The main entrance to this 12th-century fort is through the Bab Oudaia, a beautiful Moorish gateway and one of the Almohad dynasty's great architectural achievements. A simple but strong horseshoe arch flanked by two towers, it was constructed in the late 12th century by Yacoub el Mansour, probably for ceremonial rather strategic purposes.

Today a pleasant residential quarter, the kasbah occupies the site of the original *ribat* that gave the city its name. Its hilltop position made it easy to defend for the fierce Oudaia Bedouin Arabs garrisoned here by Moulay Ismail. Pass through the gate (no need for a guide: it is impossible to get lost) into the narrow main street, **Rue Djemaa**, lined with iron-studded house doors set in picturesque doorways. At the far end a terrace overlooks the fortifications, with a fine view across the Bou Regreg to Rabat's sister city, Salé. A short flight of steps leads down to the Caravelle Restaurant with a terrace overlooking the ocean.

For a restful break, return along Rue Djemaa and turn left down the Rue Bazzo to the **Café Maure**, where tables occupy a shady terrace beneath an ancient fig tree. A door from the terrace leads into the kasbah's lovely **Andalusian Garden**, planted with cypress, lemon trees, datura, roses and bougainvillaea. A stairway climbs from the garden to a 17th-century **palace** built by Moulay Ismail, well worth visiting for its vast reception rooms and delightful *hammam* (bath).

On the road downhill from the kasbah (Tarik el Marsa) is the **Oudaia Crafts Museum** (open Wed–Mon 9am–noon, 3–6pm), which has an excellent display of antique furniture, rugs and ceramics. The crafts co-operative opposite, the **Ensemble Artisanal**, sells good-quality modern work.

The Mausoleum of Mohammed V

On the eastern edge of the new town lies the nation's monument to the king who achieved independence for Morocco in 1956. Although it was built in the 1960s, the **Mausoleum of Mohammed V** (open daily 8.30am–6.30pm) is a clear celebration of traditional Moroccan craftsmanship. The entrance is flanked by guards dressed as Berber warriors. Inside you will find yourself on a mezzanine balcony beneath a magnificent carved wooden dome. On the floor below lie the sarcophagi of Mohammed V (the largest) and his two sons (Hassan II was laid to rest here in 1999). A huge bronze lamp hangs over the tombs, suspended from a ceiling that glows with rich gold ornamentation.

The mausoleum overlooks the ruins of the **Hassan Mosque**, built by the Sultan Yacoub el Mansour (Almohad dynasty) at the end of the 12th century. The Sultan died before the ambitious project was completed, and the main structure fell victim to the elements; all that remain today are the parallel ranks of stumpy columns fringed by crumbling brick walls. By contrast, the huge but unfinished minaret, now called the **Hassan Tower**, has survived unscathed, and remains as a monument to Almohad architecture. The site, set high above the banks of the Bou Regreg, is superb, and the view from the terrace is impressive.

The Archaeological Museum

Located in Rue Brihi, to the left of the huge Sounna Mosque, Rabat's **Archaeological Museum** (open Wed–Mon 9am–noon and 2.30–6pm) traces Moroccan history from prehistoric times to the Muslim conquest, with emphasis on the Phoenician and Roman eras. The collection brings together items found at Morocco's principal archaeological sites. The showpiece is the **Salle des Bronzes**, located in a separate building, which the caretaker will unlock. It contains superb bronze heads, notably of King Juba II and Cato the Younger, the Roman philosopher and statesman, as well as some exquisite statuettes, such as the Ephebus (ivy-crowned youth) and the Rider. Other rooms contain sculptures, oil lamps, figurines, jewellery, coins and other finds from Sala Colonia, Lixus and Volubilis.

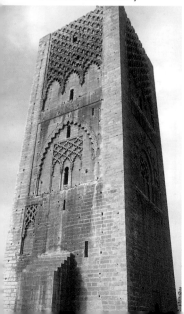

The Hassan Tower, a monument from the 12th century

The Chellah

The Roman town of Sala Colonia occupied a site that now lies just outside the walls of Rabat. The town was abandoned in 1154 in favour of Salé. The Merenids used the site as a cemetery from the 14th century, building a wall around it. This area is now known as the **Chellah** necropolis (open daily 9am–5.30pm). You enter through a dramatic

Bronze head of Juba II, found at Volubilis

Merenid gate – more ornamental than defensive, since Muslim graves contain no treasure – flanked by a pair of octagonal towers. Inside, the overgrown gardens cover the ruins of a typical provincial Roman forum, triumphal arch, porticoed market streets and a thermal bath.

Downhill from the Roman ruins is a little grove of bamboo and banana plants. On the right-hand side, behind a whitewashed tomb, is a stone basin full of crystal-clear water. In this quiet spot, childless women come and feed hard-boiled eggs to the grey eels that inhabit the pond, in the hope that ancient magic will one day bring them the gift of a son or daughter.

For a few dirhams, a guide should be able to show you around the ruined mosque next to the pond – its graceful minaret is crowned with the untidy nests of migratory storks – as well as the neighbouring *medersa* (religious school), where traces of tilework on the arches and doorways testify to its former opulence. These structures were built for holy men who were encouraged to pray and study beside the royal necropolis.

The Chellah, walled necropolis since the 14th century

Salé

The Chellah looks across the Bou Regreg to Rabat's sister city on the far bank of the river. Salé was founded in the 11th century and flourished as a trading centre in medieval times, reaching its height in the 14th century. Today it is merely a suburb of Rabat. Its past glories are recalled by several fine mosques and *medersas* (Islamic college and living quarters for students), as well as the impressive defensive walls.

The bridge across the Bou Regreg below the Hassan Tower leads to the **Bab el Mrisa** (Port Gate). Enter the gate and wander through the *mellah* (old Jewish quarter) to the busy and colourful souks that form the centre of the town. Tourists are a rare sight here: it is local people who shop here.

From the souks, Rue de la Grande Mosquée leads to Salé's **Grand Mosque**, with a tall and imposing stone doorway at the top of a flight of steps. You cannot enter the mosque unless you are a Muslim, but you can visit its former religious college, just opposite. Although on a small scale, the lovely 14th-century **Medersa of Abu el Hassan** (temporarily closed for renovation) is as finely wrought and well preseved as its larger counterparts in Fez and Meknes. Above the walls decorated with coloured *zellige* tiles are carved cedar screens and delicate plaster-work, among the finest in Morocco.

The stairway leading to the roof passes two floors of tiny rooms that served as lodgings for the theological students who studied here. From the top of the stairs you can see into the courtyard of the mosque next door; there is also a superb panorama of Rabat, Salé and the river from here.

You can return to Rabat by ferry. Just follow the crowds to the river below Bab el Khebaz, where rowing boats await.

CASABLANCA

In 1515 the Portuguese built a small town on the Atlantic coast of Morocco and named it Casa Branca ('White House'). Spanish merchants settling here in the 18th century called it Casablanca, and it remained a backwater until it was occupied by the French in 1907. Under the Protectorate it grew to become Morocco's busiest port, its most populous city and the economic and industrial capital of the kingdom, accounting for more than half of the country's industrial output. (In Arabic, the city is called Dar el Baida – 'White House'– but most Moroccans refer to it as 'Casa'.)

Orientation

Casablanca has a population of around 3.3 million, making it one of Africa's largest cities. The heart of modern Casablanca is **Place des Nations Unies**, where all the thoroughfares converge beneath the facade of the Hyatt Regency Hotel. A wasteland in the early 1900s, it is now a busy conglomeration of offices, banks, restaurants, hotels and shops.

The Grand Mosque of Hassan II is open to non-Muslims

Situated just off the square is the entrance to the **Old Medina**, which is less exotic than the colourful souks in Fez or Marrakesh.

South of the square is the city's administrative hub, **Place Mohammed V**, with the City Hall, the law courts, the French Consulate, the post office and the Sacré Coeur Cathedral (all grand examples of 1930s Mauresque architecture), as well as wonderful parks. Near the cathedral at 30 Boulevard Brahim Roudani is the Villa des Arts (open Tues–Sat 11am–7pm), an exhibition centre for contemporary art.

About 1km (½ mile) south-west of the centre is the **New Medina** (Quartier Habous), built by the French as a model medina in the 1930s, and a good place to buy souvenirs, pastries and clothes.

The Hassan II Mosque

Casablanca's most impressive sight is without doubt the **Grand Mosque of Hassan II** (guided tours Sat–Thur 9am, 10am, 11am and 2pm), completed in 1994. The world's biggest mosque outside Mecca, its prayer hall can accommodate up to 25,000 faithful and another 80,000 in the courtyard. The building cost over $1 billion, raised entirely by public subscription, with all Moroccans contributing according to their means. The mosque's interior is a *tour de force* of Moroccan architectural motifs and craftsmanship, amplified by the grandeur and size of the structure. A glass elevator climbs the side of the minaret which soars 210 metres (689ft) and is topped at night with a green laser beam pointing towards Mecca.

West of the mosque is the rather untidy Corniche, with restaurants, hotels, swimming pools and nightclubs popular with tourists and locals, which ends at the fine sandy beach and white houses of **Aïn Diab**.

You can return to town via **Anfa**, an exclusive residential quarter whose luxurious villas are the finest in Casablanca.

MEKNES (MEKNÈS)

▶ **Meknes** was founded in the 10th century by a Berber tribe called the Meknassa, but it was the Alaouite Sultan Moulay Ismail who put the city on the map when he chose it as the site for his new capital in the late 17th century. Both as a governor and a Sultan Moulay Ismail was a man of excesses. A ruthless tyrant, he had a harem of 500 wives and concubines and fathered hundreds of children. He was also a great admirer of France's Louis XIV, and set about building an imperial city to rival the Palace of Versailles. Christian slaves and local tribesmen laboured for years to realise Ismail's grandiose plan, which comprised a complex of 24 royal palaces with mosques, barracks and ornamental gardens, surrounded by four sets of massive defensive walls. Following the death of Moulay Ismail, his city fell into ruin, but the 20th century brought restoration and rejuvenation.

> ### Non, merci!
>
> A great admirer of Louis XIV, Moulay Ismail recommended the Muslim faith to the French king and asked for the hand of his daughter in marriage. Both proposals were politely refused.

The Ville Nouvelle

Most visitors stay in the new town, where the majority of the comfortable hotels are concentrated. The area is a bit of a jumble, and lacks the order and sweeping boulevards of its neighbour to the east, Fez, but Meknes is generally more low-key, and many of its residents are extremely helpful to visitors.

A grand panorama can be enjoyed at the four-star Hotel Transatlantique *(see page 129)*. From its hilltop vantage point you can look across the Boufekrane valley to the walls, rooftops and minarets of Meknes's old medina, ranged along the heights.

The Imperial City

The old **Imperial City** is so extensive that it can be tiring to 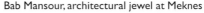 explore it all on foot – you should allow at least three hours. If you don't want to walk, you can take a tour by bus or ask a taxi driver to drive you to the principal sights.

From the new town, Avenue Moulay Ismail crosses a bridge over the valley of the Oued Boufekrane. Follow the road that circles the medina to arrive at Place el Hedim at the entrance to the old city. The square is a popular meeting place, with fancy street lamps, fountains and a mock-Andalusian arcade housing shops and cafés.

Dominating the southern end of the square is the monumental gateway of **Bab Mansour**, the crowning jewel of Moulay Ismail's architectural legacy. Intricately decorated with richly coloured tiles, it marks the entrance to the vast precincts of the imperial court. Right of the Bab Mansour

Bab Mansour, architectural jewel at Meknes

Geometric mosaic patterns on the tomb of Moulay Ismail

is a smaller gate in very similar style, the Bab Jamaa en Nouar.

Go through the Bab Mansour to the great expanse of Place Lalla Aouda; a second gate, the Bab el Filala, leads to another square. The small, domed building just to your right is the **Koubbet el Khayatine** (open daily 9am–noon and 3–6pm), where Ismail used to receive foreign ambassadors. A stairway beneath the pavilion leads to subterranean vaults which are said to have served as a **prison** for the European slaves who laboured on the construction of the imperial city. It is claimed that the underground chambers ran for over 7km (4 miles) and that up to 40,000 slaves were incarcerated here each night in total darkness (the tiny windows were made by the French).

The Tomb of Moulay Ismail

On the far side of the square an archway leads to the triple-arched entrance to the **Tomb of Moulay Ismail** (open daily 8am–12.30pm and 3pm–6pm). The doorway is magnificent; like the rest of the tomb complex it was renovated in the 1950s by Moulay Ismail's Alaouite descendant Mohammed V. From here, several elegant courtyards lead to the main enclosure (grass mats at its threshold remind you to leave your shoes here, as the mosque-tomb is a sacred place of pilgrimage and prayer). While non-Muslims are not admitted to the inner sanctuary they can enter the ante-chamber, which offers glimpses of the tomb. Resting beneath sumptuously decorated horseshoe arches, it is watched over by four ornate grandfather clocks, gifts to Moulay Ismail from Louis XIV when he refused to grant the sultan his daughter's hand in marriage.

On leaving the tomb, turn left and follow the road through the left-hand arch of the **Bab er Rih** (Gate of the Wind) to emerge into a forbidding 800m- (875-yd-) long corridor squeezed in between two mighty walls. Behind the wall to the right is the **Dar el Makhzen**, still a Royal Palace (closed to visitors), though Mohammed VI rarely stays in Meknes.

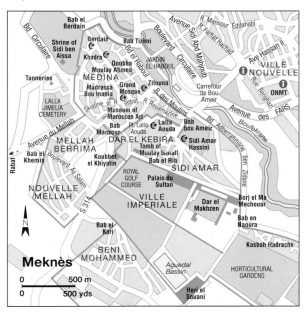

At the far end, turn right past the main entrance to the Royal Palace and continue through another gate to the **Dar el Ma**, also known as the **Heri es Souani** (open daily 9am–noon and 3–6pm). This large 17th-century high-vaulted building served both as a granary and feed store for the 12,000 steeds in Moulay Ismail's vast stables. Take the stairs to the pleasant rooftop café-garden, with a fine view of the city and the huge Aguedal Basin, once used to irrigate the imperial city's gardens. The remains of Moulay Ismail's stables are attached to the granary.

Nearby to the south stands the **Dar el Beida**, a thick-walled fortress. Built as a sultan's palace in the late 18th century, it is now a military academy.

The Medina

Across Place el Hedim from the Bab Mansour is a gate into the **medina**; beside it is the gate of the **Dar Jamaï**, the 19th-century former private palace of a minister of state and now home to the excellent **Museum of Moroccan Arts** (open

Moroccan Wines

The low hills around Meknes are the main centre of Morocco's wine industry. Set up by the French, as in Tunisia and Algeria, wine production continues despite the Koran's ban on alcohol. The red wines are generally better than the whites. Among the best reds are the widely available Médaillon and Cuvée Première du Président. Les Cépages de Meknes is also palatable. Among the whites often found on wine lists are Oustalet and Cuvée Président Sauvignon Blanc. One of the best lighter wines is Gris de Boulaouane, a fruity grey-rosé produced near Casablanca.

Although available in Europe, Moroccan wines are rarely on sale in the medinas. You should go instead to an upmarket grocery or supermarket in the *ville nouvelle* (new town) of a city. Note that many restaurants do not serve alcohol during the month of Ramadan.

daily 9am–noon and 3–6pm). The museum's impressive collections include typical Fez and Meknes pottery, silk embroidery, carpets from the Middle Atlas, ceramic tiles, jewellery and wrought-ironwork. The lavish architecture of the palace itself is also worth seeing.

An alley to the right of the Dar Jamai leads to the **Grand Mosque**. The most sacred and important of the city's mosques, it has elaborate entrances, ornate gates, red-tiled cupolas and roof, and a green-tiled minaret.

Across the street from the mosque is the **Bou Inania Medersa** (open 9am–noon and 3–6pm), built in the 14th century to rival the Bou Inania Medersa in Fez. The exquisite Koran school is richly decorated with *zellige* tiles and stucco. Go up to the roof for an excellent view of the mosque and medina.

The Dar el Ma, the city's former granary

As you explore the maze of streets in the medina, you'll encounter the mingled scents of sweet incense, tangy citrus fruit, aromatic wood from the joiners' shops, and grilling meat from the numerous food stalls. Near the Grand Mosque, huge blue doors mark the entrance to the **Kissaria el Dlala**, a souk specialising in blankets and *jellabas* (traditional kaftans). It is usually crowded (except on Fridays) with men attending the auction of blankets and garments.

Along Rue du Souk en Nejjarin (woodworkers' souk), a small number of modern stores break the solid ranks of traditional carpentry shops. Throughout the medina you will find carpet shops housed in magnificent, once-great private mansions, worth visiting for their architecture alone.

Excursions from Meknes

About 30km (19 miles) north of Meknes lies **Volubilis** (open daily 9am–noon and 2.30–6pm), the former capital of the Roman province of Mauretania Tingitana and now the site of the most extensive and impressive Roman ruins in Morocco. You can hire a grand taxi in Meknes to take you to both Volubilis and nearby Moulay Idriss. If you have your own transport follow the road to Tangier for 15km (10 miles), then turn right on a minor road. Soon the ruins come into view, set on a triangular plateau abutting the foothills of the Zerhoun massif.

> **Deserted city**
>
> In the 3rd century Volubilis had a population of about 20,000. Most of the ruins date from this time. By the 4th century the Romans had left.

Volubilis was a flourishing Roman city from the time of Christ until the end of the 3rd century, when the Romans began to withdraw from Morocco, but it remained an outpost of Christian culture until the Arab conquest in the 7th century. It was a rich and prosperous place, and many vestiges of its heyday survive.

A Tour of the Ruins at Volubilis

From the café and open-air museum at the entrance, take the path across a bridge to the ruins. Volubilis is small and easy to cover, but be aware that there is very little shade on the site. The most important remains are clearly labelled and red arrows point the way. After passing a number of olive-oil presses – olives were central to the economy of Volubilis – you reach the **House of Orpheus**, a luxurious Roman villa containing mosaics of Orpheus, the Chariot of Amphitrite and the Nine Dolphins. Beyond, a broad, paved street takes you past the 3rd-century **Baths of Galienus**, originally the most lavish public baths in the city, to the modestly proportioned **Forum**, where the remains of the **Capitol** and the **Basilica** dominate the site.

Ahead is the massive **Triumphal Arch**, built in honour of the Emperor Caracalla. An inscription suggests that it was once topped by a huge chariot and horses. The arch marks the western end of the city's main street, Decumanus Maximus, where ruts worn by cart wheels can still be seen in parts of the stone paving. The remains of villas lining this street contain many fine and extraordinarily well preserved **mosaics**. The splendour of the villas indicates that Volubilis

The Triumphal Arch, built to honour Emperor Caracalla

Fine mosaic floor in the
House of Orpheus, Volubilis

was a cultured, prosperous town – as do the superb bronzes recovered from the site, which are now on display in the Salle des Bronzes in the Archaeological Museum in Rabat *(see page 40)*.

Moulay Idriss

Located barely 3km (2 miles) from Volubilis, the holy town of **Moulay Idriss** tumbles down the slopes of its twin hills, Khiber and Tasga. Between the two peaks lies the **Mausoleum of Moulay Idriss I**, the 8th-century founder of Morocco's first Arab dynasty. For much of the year the town is a sleepy backwater, but in September it is the focus for an annual *moussem* (holy festival), when thousands of pilgrims gather at the shrine of Morocco's first sultan. At one time Christians were barred from visiting the town itself. Today the shrine and the mosque are still barred to non-Muslims, and visitors are not allowed to stay overnight in the town.

The main square, the busiest part of the town, has several pleasant cafés and is lined with shops and stalls selling religious artifacts, decorated candles and giant poles of locally produced coloured nougat – items traditionally sold in the vicinity of a tomb in Muslim places of pilgrimage.

The entrance to Moulay Idriss's shrine is at the far end of the square. Here, a wooden bar across the passage reiterates the following warning: 'No entry to non-Muslims'. One of the many unofficial guides to be found in the square will lead you up the steep alleyways of the Khiber to a well-known viewpoint, the Terrace of Sidi Abdallah el Hajjam.

Excursions into the Middle Atlas

A number of destinations in the quiet, forested mountains of the Middle Atlas make for easy day-trips from either Meknes or Fez. **Azrou**, about 50km (30 miles) southeast of Meknes, is known for its carpet and weaving cooperative. The European-style mountain town of **Ifrane**, just northeast of Azrou, on the Fez-Azrou road, is unlike any other town in Morocco, with expensive summer villas, built as cool, tranquil retreats from the blazing summer of the interior; it is also home to Al Akhawayn University, founded in 1995. A road from Ifrane leads to the small ski resort of **Mischliffin**: two ski lifts operate during the winter season when snow depths are sufficient.

Sefrou *(see box below)* is a small ancient walled city 30km (19 miles) south of Fez (one hour by bus or *grand taxi*). At its high altitude Sefrou can provide a cool day trip away from the brutally hot summer days of Fez and Meknes.

Cherry Festival City

In the foothills of the Middle Atlas, surrounded by cherry orchards, is the old walled city of Sefrou. Until the 1960s the town was host to a large community of Morocco's Jews – as is evident from the architecture: the *mellah* (Jewish quarter) is still characterised by their houses with wooden balconies. The River Aggaï dissects the medieval white-walled medina, which comes to life on Thursdays when peasants from the surrounding hills come to town for the weekly market.

Renowned for its abundant fruit, Sefrou hosts an annual festival at the end of June to mark the cherry harvest. The cherry festival draws visitors from all over Morocco to take part in its folkloric spectacles.

In the hills to the east of Sefrou more than 50 varieties of olive are cultivated – and the locals have at least as many different delicious ways of preparing them.

FEZ (FÈS)

▶ **Fez** is one of the greatest and best preserved medieval Islamic cities in the world. For centuries it attracted and nourished a community of poets, musicians and intellectuals that included the great Tunisian-born historian and social commentator Ibn Khaldoun (1332–1406) and the young Moses Maimonides (1135–1204), who later became an eminent doctor and philosopher at the court of Sultan

▶ Saladin in Egypt. **Fez el Bali**, the medina, is filled with fine examples of Islamic architecture and artistry. Many treasures were created by successive waves of artisans fleeing the Christian reconquest of El Andalús in southern Spain. The medina is not merely a historical site, but also a living city, where craftsmen, souks and a good portion of the city's population thrive in a style that has existed for more than 1,000 years.

Dried fruit in Old Fez

Along with other international treasures, Fez has been declared a World Heritage Site. A huge restoration programme to preserve the long-neglected buildings and infrastructure of the medina of Fez has been launched by the Moroccan government together with UNESCO and international private foundations and organisations.

Many *medersas*, *fondouks* (storehouses) and palaces under renovation will be only partially open in the next few years. In parallel, special efforts are being made to preserve the unique way of life in Fez el Bali, so that the medina will continue to be a vital, living community.

Babouches

Babouches, the hand-sewn pointed slippers for which Fez is famed, are made from three types of leather: the upper is calf skin, the lining goat hide and the sole a thicker leather from the animal's head.

The oldest of Morocco's four imperial cities, Fez is really three cities in one. Fez el Bali (Old Fez) was founded by Moulay Idriss II at the end of the 8th century. Five hundred years later, the Merinid sultans added many jewels of Hispano-Moorish architecture to the old city and built Fez el Jdid (New Fez) outside the walls. Then, during the 20th century, the French built a modern city, the Ville Nouvelle, about 2km (1½ miles) to the west.

The Ville Nouvelle

Most visitors arrive first in the Ville Nouvelle, where the railway station, bus station, tourist office and many hotels and restaurants are concentrated. There is little to see here, but it's a pleasant place to get your bearings, and plan your exploration of Fez el Bali.

The majestic, palm-lined **Avenue Hassan II** is the main axis of the modern town (tourist office on Place de la Résistance). The best cafés, restaurants and shops are along the tree-lined **Avenue Mohammed V**, which is at its liveliest in the early evening, when the whole town turns out to promenade and sit on the café terraces. Avenue de la Liberté joins the Tour de Fès, an attractive ring road that encircles the old city. At least once during your stay, take a taxi ride around it *(see page 66)* to get a feel of the old city's size and complexity.

Fez el Jdid

From the tourist office on the Place de la Résistance, Boulevard Moulay Youssef leads to the open space of **Place du Commerce**, the gateway to Fez el Jdid. In the far right corner of the square a small gate marks the way into the crowded streets of the *mellah*, the old Jewish quarter. Take a stroll down Grande Rue du Mellah, lined with shops selling household goods and food. At the far end, cross the main street, then pass through the Bab Semmarin into **Grande Rue de Fès el Jdid**, a busy shopping thoroughfare. At the end of the street, an archway on the left leads into a high-walled enclosure. Turn right through a gate for Avenue des Français, leading to the Bab Boujeloud and Fez el Bali.

Fez el Bali

Many first-time visitors may want to wander with the flow of the medina (the main roads lead steadily downhill, towards the Kairaouine Mosque, at the heart of Fez el Bali); others prefer to employ a guide. However independent you may be, at some point a guide can be useful to get you into *medersas*, historical sites and out-of-the-way parts of the medina, and to provide background information. Licensed guides can be hired from the tourist offices *(see page 126)* and from any of the larger hotels.

The medina of Fez is traditionally entered through the **Bab Boujeloud**, a blue-tiled monumental gate built by the French in 1913 at the junction of Fez el Bali and Fez el Jdid. The two major arteries of the Old City – the **Talaa Seghira** (in front of you) and the **Talaa Kebira** (slightly to your left) – lead from the Bab Boujeloud into the depths of the medina. The beginning of the Talaa Seghira is lined with restaurants that are good for an inexpensive meal, and with stalls selling wedges of semolina cake, flat bread and savoury snacks. For a first visit, follow the more interesting Talaa Kebira through

Bab Boujeloud marks the entrance to the medina in Fez

the shaded, smoky meat and olive bazaars. In a few minutes you will come to the Bou Inania Medersa (on your right), the most beautiful of Morocco's religious buildings open to tourists.

The **Bou Inania Medersa** (open 9am–5.30pm), a college for Koranic studies, was built in the 1350s by the Merinid Sultan Bou Inan to rival the power of the Kairaouine Mosque and University. The building is one of the glories of Hispano-Moorish architecture. Intensely complex, sumptuous but orderly designs in carved cedar, hand-cut *zellige* tiles and sculpted stucco cover the walls of the courtyard. The serene proportions of the courtyard help unite the intricate decorations, reflecting belief in the unity and order underlying the complicated universe. In the centre of the onyx-and-marble paved courtyard is a fountain; carved cedar screens cover the lecture alcoves in which the boys studied. The large alcove on the far side of the courtyard (facing towards

The Bou Inania Medersa, founded in 1350

Mecca) is a prayer hall covered by an intricate ceiling.

The upper storeys contain a network of student cells, offering views over the courtyard from the windows with their pierced wooden screens. If you are allowed upstairs to see the students' tiny rooms, notice the little slot beside each door: it was not for mail, but for the daily ration of unleavened bread. There is also a great view of the city from the rooftop.

As you leave the *medersa* and return to the Talaa Kebira, look up across the street and to the left. This is the site of a curious waterclock; a beautiful contraption of metal bowls and finely carved wood, which was one of the wonders of medieval Fez. Although the woodwork was recently restored, the clock has not worked for more than 500 years. With the operational plans lost, nobody really knows how it functioned.

As you walk down the Talaa Kebira, look for old *fondouks* opening off the street. These two- to four-storey buildings with courtyards lined with small rooms are an integral part of the medina. Built at about the same time as the *medersa*, they once provided accommodation for travelling merchants and their caravans. Today they are used as workshops and warehouses by local craftsmen and traders in the souk.

Continuing along the Talaa Kebira, at the foot of a hill, you will find the **Souk el Attarine** (the perfume or spice market). Pause here to look over the shops full of spices, cosmetic and herbal goods – tree bark and incense, snake skins, twigs, roots, charms and potions are all on sale. Among the traditional herbalist shops are some specialising in souvenirs and Moroccan crafts. A few are set up in beautiful old mansions, and a shopping expedition here gives you the bonus of a tour through a traditional Moroccan house. Just off Souk el Attarine is the shady **Souk el Henna**, where you can buy henna leaves and powder, *kohl* and other cosmetics.

The first side-street to the right, just before the Dar Saada restaurant, leads to the **Zaouia of Moulay Idriss II**. This structure, containing the tomb of the founder of Fez and son of the first Moroccan Arab sovereign, is the most revered sanctuary in Morocco. Entry is forbidden to non-Muslims, but you can go past the wooden bar that marks the outer limits of the *horm* (sacred area) and peer up the steps to the magnificent doors of the prayer room and the glittering

The Fountains of Fez

Fez owes its numerous fountains to the vision of the Almoravid Sultan Youssef Ben Tashfine, who re-routed the river to achieve his aim. Engineers were instructed to create an elaborate system of channels and by the late 11th century every mosque, *medersa*, *fondouk*, street fountain and public bath, as well as most of the richer households, had water. The system included an effective method of flushing the drains. The sound and sight of Fez's many drinking fountains refresh the senses. Wear, tear and pollution have dulled their brilliant *zellige* (mosaic) decoration and in some cases destroyed the pipes feeding the fountains but, thanks to an ambitious restoration programme, 42 of Fez's historic drinking fountains are being restored to their former glory.

chandeliers beyond – you must refrain from taking photographs, however. The *zaouia* (centre of a religious brotherhood) dates from the 9th century, but was rebuilt during the 13th and 18th centuries.

The Great Mosque

Returning to the Talaa Kebira and Souk el Attarine, you approach the richest concentration of historic buildings in Fez. This is one of the oldest parts of the city, its foundation dating back some 1,000 years. The greatest architectural jewel of the quarter is the **Kairaouine Mosque**, built in the late 9th century on the orders of a woman refugee from Kairouan, in Tunisia. Enlarged and embellished over the centuries, and dazzling in the richness and detail of its decoration, it can accommodate approximately 20,000 worshippers.

The Kairaouine Mosque, jewel of the medina

The mosque is also the seat of the **Kairaouine University**, one of the oldest in the world (most non-theological divisions of the university were moved to Rabat after 1956). Although non-Muslims may not enter the mosque itself, its 14 gates allow a view of the ornate doorways and a glimpse of the vast interior.

The streets around the mosque are home to a number of *medersas*. Built in 1325, near the souk of the same name, the **El Attarine Medersa** (open daily, 8.30am–5pm; temporarily closed for renovation) is smaller than the Bou Inania Medersa, but similar in design and equally beautiful. From its roof there is a fine view of the courtyard and minarets of the Kairaouine Mosque. Following the walls of the Kairaouine clockwise from El Attarine, you soon pass the **Misbahiya Medersa** (built in 1346). The *medersa* is now semi-derelict, but it has a particularly pretty central fountain imported from Spain during the Saadian dynasty.

Dyers and Tanners

Continuing round the Kairaouine walls you soon find yourself in enchanting tree-shaded **Place es Seffarine** (brass- and copper-workers' square). Beyond the lower end of the square a small bridge crosses the Oued (River) Fez. Just before the bridge, through a gate on the right, is **Rue des Teinturiers** (dyers' street), usually strung with brightly coloured swathes of wool and cotton hanging out to dry.

Follow the river towards the *quartier des tanneurs* (the **Tanners' Quarter**), and you come to an area that has hardly changed since medieval times. Semi-clad boy workers tread the skins in earthen vats filled with chemicals or dyes, and stack the reeking hides on to donkeys for delivery to the leather-workers' shops. The bridge by the Tanners' Quarter is known as the **Bein El Moudoun** ('the bridge between the cities'), as it links the two oldest quarters of Fez. For a few

Earthen vats filled with dyes in the Tanners' Quarter

dirhams you'll be able to get access to one of the roof terraces overlooking the working area.

Andalusian Quarter

Cross the bridge into **Fez el Andalous**, the Andalusian quarter, and follow the main street (Rue Seftah) uphill until you reach a lofty portal at the top of a long flight of steps. This marks the entrance of the **Andalusian Mosque**, founded and endowed by a sister of the woman who established the Kairaouine Mosque. You will notice that it is quite different from its counterparts across the river. There is a special boldness in the design which seems both foreign and exotic. The main door, built by an Almohad sultan in the early 1200s, is all there is to see for most visitors, because entry is forbidden to non-Muslims. Down the street to the right of the door is the **Medersa Es Sahrij** (open daily 9.30am–noon and 3–6pm), which dates from 1320 and is richly decorated.

Back at Place Seffarine, you can cross the bridge by the Rue des Teinturiers, turn right, and in a few minutes reach Place Er Rsif, where a *petit taxi* can take you back to the Ville Nouvelle. Alternatively, continue to the far end of the Rue des Teinturiers and turn right into the covered passage of the Rue Cherratin, passing the Medersa es Cherratin, to reach the back of the Zaouia of Moulay Idriss II gateway. Here you will find the **women's entrance to the sanctuary**. The polychrome and gilt decoration of the facade is breathtaking. The copper plate below the window, covered with fancy wrought-iron work, once had a hole (now covered over) into which women could insert an arm to 'catch' the saint's blessing. The saint lies at rest on the other side of the window.

Beyond the sanctuary is **Place Nejjarine** (Joiners' Square), the centre of Fez's cabinet- and furniture-making industry. The fountain built for the joiners, an exquisite example of Moorish decorative art, has been restored using ancient mosaic techniques. Beside the fountain, the beautifully restored 18th-century **Fondouk Nejjarine** now contains a **Museum of the Wooden Arts** (open daily 10am–6pm), although the building itself is the museum's greatest exhibit.

Follow the street to the right of the fountain, which eventually leads uphill to the Talaa Seghira, and to the Bab Boujeloud. Nearby is **Dar Batha Museum** (open Sat–Mon, Wed–Thur 9am–noon and 2.30pm–6pm, Fri 9am–11.30am and 3–6pm), where Moroccan arts are on show in a 19th-century mansion. You cannot visit the Royal Palace in Fez, but the palatial Dar Batha, surrounded by fascinating gardens, will give you some idea of how the city's upper classes lived a hundred years ago. The ceremonial chambers are now exhibition rooms in which you can find everything from medieval astrolabes to local carpets and costumes.

A Drive Around Fez

A good way to get an idea of the city's layout is to drive along the **Route du Tour de Fès**, a simple 16-km (10-mile) circuit that surrounds Fez el Bali and Fez el Jdid and offers vast, commanding views from the heights to the north. Alternatively, take a taxi to the **Borj Nord** (North Fort), above the bus station; this 16th-century fortress now houses a small **Museum of Arms**. From here there is a lovely view across the rooftops of Fez el Bali, in the valley below, with the roof of the Kairaouine Mosque prominent in the centre. On the hillside behind the mosque, just above the Palais Jamai Hotel, are the crumbling **Merinid Tombs** dating from the final years of the Merinid Dynasty.

MARRAKESH (MARRAKECH)

Marrakesh is the gateway to the desert, the meeting and marketplace of African, Berber and Arab Morocco, a city of tranquillity and throbbing intensity. The city's red *pisé* (dried mud) walls rise from the red earth, glowing in the late afternoon sun; the vast souks, the best in Morocco, are filled with customers; the drums of the Jemaa el Fna, the central square, summon crowds to a daily circus of fortune tellers, musicians, story-tellers, snake charmers and food vendors. Yet visitors to this fiery city can walk to the edge of the medina and find peaceful gardens and olive groves stretching to the snow-capped Atlas Mountain peaks in the distance.

Dynamic city

With a population of just over a million, Marrakesh is Morocco's third largest city after Casablanca and Rabat. Flourishing industries make it a fast-growing economic centre. Low labour costs and its strategic position explain the increasing number of foreign enterprises that are setting up in the city.

The fourth of Morocco's imperial cities, Marrakesh was founded in 1062 by Yusuf ibn Tashfin and served as the capital under the Almoravid and Almohad dynasties until 1269, and then again under the Saadians in the 16th century. Visiting Europeans mispronounced its name as 'Marrak', and thus the city gave its name to the kingdom that came to be known as Morocco.

The walls of Marrakesh

Today Marrakesh is the commercial centre for the High Atlas and the Moroccan Sahara. It is also a prime destination for European tourists in search of sun all year round. The ancient medina is flanked by the new town of **Guéliz**, a pleasant city of wide boulevards and planned urban neighbourhoods. Here you will find the more expensive cafés, modern hotels, shops and restaurants, car-rental agencies, banks and airline offices. The centre of interest for visitors to Marrakesh, however, is the medina and the famous Jemaa el Fna.

Jemaa el Fna

Near the eastern end of Avenue Mohammed V stands the city's most notable landmark, the 70-metre- (230-ft) high **Koutoubia Minaret**. The finest of the three great 12th-century Almohad minarets – the others are the Giralda in Seville and the unfinished Hassan Tower in Rabat *(see page 40)* –

it established the classical proportions of subsequent minarets in Morocco. Each face of the Koutoubia presents a different decorative pattern; its exquisite, subtle ceramics can only testify to the former splendour of its decoration.

The street opposite the minaret leads into the wide open space of **Jemaa el Fna** (the assembly or parade of the dead), one of the world's most animated city squares. This name hardly seems appropriate for the endless pageant of activity that unfolds here. Indeed, the precise meaning of Jemaa el Fna is unclear; the name most likely dates from the time when the heads of those who had displeased the Almoravid or Almohad sultans were displayed in the square.

Jemaa el Fna is the heart of traditional Marrakesh. If possible, arrive just before darkness falls, when the Koutoubia Minaret is silhouetted against a pink and crimson sky, and the crowds mill thicker than ever. You will see street entertainment

The show never stops in North Africa's most animated square

at its best – groups of Berber musicians and dancers, fire-eaters, sword-swallowers, acrobats snake-charmers, storytellers and boxers. Performers lead their monkeys and lizards past stalls selling orange juice, roasted chick peas, peanuts, hard-boiled eggs, sweet fritters, kebabs

and *tajines*. Around the edges of the square are scribes, travelling dentists, henna tattooists, traditional doctors with potions and amulets, and grinning barbers wielding their cut-throat razors. When you need to take refuge, there are plenty of cafés bordering the square, some of which have rooftop terraces offering a grandstand view of the proceedings.

The Souks

The **souks** of the medina spread northwards from the Jemaa el Fna. They are at their busiest in the early morning and late afternoon, the most interesting times to visit. A guide is not really necessary, but having one will make things easier if your time is limited. Official guides can be hired from the tourist office *(see page 126)* or any of the larger hotels.

The main entrance to the souks is at the opposite end of the square from the Koutoubia Minaret. The alley opposite the Café de France and left of the Restaurant al Fath will take you to **Rue Souk Smarine**, the main thoroughfare, typically striped with sunshine and shadow, and lined with the most expensive craft and antiques shops. Where the street forks, bear right. Immediately on the right, a narrow lane leads into the **Rahba Qedima**, a square with spice shops and the great Café des Épices *(see page 140)*. Stallholders here will demonstrate the spices, roots and herbs used in medicine, magic and cosmetics: mandrake root is an aphrodisiac; argan oil is good for massage; the mineral antimonite, finely ground, produces kohl to outline the eyes; and countless jars hold arcane objects used in magic spells. Off the Rahba Qedima on the same side as the Café des Épices is the **Criée Berbère** (Souk Zrabia), the former slave market, where carpets from the Middle Atlas are auctioned in the afternoon.

Back on the main street, Souk el Kebir, you soon reach the **Kissaria** (covered street markets) in the heart of the souk, where a variety of goods are for sale. Further on, your nose will guide you to the **Souk Cherratin** (leather market), where the shops are packed with jackets, bags, purses, sandals and boots.

The bustle of the souks

Head left through the leather souk, then turn right to reach an open space with a domed shrine on the right, the **Koubba Baddiyin**. This 12th-century small ablutions chamber opposite the Ben Youssef mosque is the city's only surviving Almoravid building.

Medersa and Museum

The next street on the right follows the wall of the Ben Youssef Mosque; turn left at the far end and look for the discreet entrance to the **Ben Youssef Medersa** (open daily 9am–6pm). Established in the 14th century, this religious school was rebuilt in Andalusian style by the Saadians in the 16th century. The largest *medersa* in Morocco, it was built to rival those in Fez. The main courtyard is bordered on two sides by delicate arcades, and a beautiful cupola of carved cedarwood surmounts the prayer room at the end of the courtyard. The school's 130 or so cells would have accommodated several hundred students.

Andalusian style: the
Ben Youssef Medersa

Nearby, the 19th-century **Palais Mnebbi**, beautifully restored in the 1990s, now houses the **Museum of Marrakesh** (open daily 9.30am–6pm). The collection ranges across eight centuries of Moroccan art and crafts and includes superb examples of Islamic calligraphy, as well as ceramics, illuminated manuscripts and, in the former *hammam*, 18th- and 19th-century lithographs and watercolours of Morocco. Occasional exhibitions of contemporary Moroccan paintings are held here.

More Souks

Not far from here is the **Souk Haddadine** (blacksmiths' souk). Then, on your return to the Jemaa el Fna, you go through the **Souk des Babouches** (slipper market). Close by is the **Souk Chouari** (woodworkers' souk), where the heady scent of thuya wood and cedar perfumes the air. Turning left along Rue Souk Attarine, you soon come to the **Souk des Teinturiers** (dyers' souk), hung with brightly

coloured skeins of freshly dyed wool and silk drying in the sun, creating a patchwork of colours. To the west is the **Mouassine Mosque**, built by the Saadians in the 16th century.

Rue Souk Attarine leads back to the Jemaa el Fna. A less-used entrance to the souk, **Rue el Mouassine** starts from the corner of Jemaa el Fna near the Café Argana. Mouassine has become one of the more fashionable quarters to shop in, with good-quality craft and antiques shops, often at more reasonable prices than the main souk.

Entrance to the Saadian Tombs, a long-forgotten resting place

The Medina

The part of the medina south of Jemaa el Fna contains a number of splendid monuments to the dynasties that once ruled Morocco. Follow Rue du Bab Agnaou south from Jemaa el Fna to Bab er Rob, a huge gate in the city wall. Go left through another gate, the ancient **Bab Agnaou**, and you will see the Mosque el Mansour ahead. To its right is the narrow entrance to the magnificent **Saadian Tombs** (open daily 8.30–11.45am and 2.30–5.45pm). Built by Ahmed el Mansour in the 16th century, the Saadian Tombs were walled up about 100 years later by the vengeful Sultan Moulay Ismail. They lay forgotten until 1917, when French aerial photographs revealed their existence. A passageway was cut through the wall to allow tourists to admire the sumptuous pavilions where the Saadian imperial families lie buried. Most impressive is the **Room of the Twelve Columns**, where the tombs of Ahmed el Mansour, his son and his grandson are marked by marble slabs. The sobriety of the cedarwood cupola contrasts with the exuberance of the walls, decorated with *zellige* mosaics and stucco.

Another walk south from Jemaa el Fna, down either the colourful Rue Riad Zeitoun Kedim or the equally fascinating Rue Riad Zeitoun Jedid, leads to Place des Ferblantiers. To the right of the square is the ruined, late 16th-century **El Badi Palace** (open daily 8.30–11.45am and 2.30–5.45pm). Once the residence of Ahmed el Mansour, it was stripped of its wealth and largely destroyed by the jealous Sultan Moulay Ismail, but the sheer scale of the place is still impressive.

A few minutes' walk from the Place des Ferblantiers brings you to the **Bahia Palace** (open 8.30–11.45am and 2.30–

Riad Fever

The fever for renovating *riads* in Marrakesh's medina has resulted in over 600 registered guesthouses catering to all budgets. Many cost the same as a hotel and some are incredibly luxurious. With four or five rooms, *riads* are more intimate than hotels, the service is more personal and though always close to the lively souks, they are usually tranquil places. They all serve a Moroccan breakfast, with fresh orange juice, pancakes and croissants, and most provide home-cooked dinner on request. Many *riads* are hidden deep in the medina; when you arrive in the city arrange to meet someone from the *riad* at a nearby landmark.

Agencies that specialise in *riad* rental include the following: Marrakech Medina (tel: 024 44 24 48, <www.marrakech-medina.com>), Marrakech Riads (tel: 024 42 64 63, <www.marrakech-riads.net>) and Riads au Maroc (tel: 024 43 19 00, <www.riadomaroc.com>).

5.45pm, Fri 8.45–11.30am and 3–5.45pm), the residence of Si Ahmed Ben Mousa, Chief Vizier to Sultan Moulay el Hassan, built at the end of the 19th century. A guide will lead you through luxurious apartments to the harem, a beautiful courtyard with separate chambers for the vizier's four wives. A garden of palms, cypress and ivy in the centre of the court has fountains and a delightful gazebo.

Nearby is **Dar Si Said** (walk north up Rue Riad Zitoun el Jdid and turn right). This grand palace, built by the same family as the Bahia, now houses the excellent **Museum of Moroccan Arts** (open Wed–Mon 9am–12.15pm and 3–6.15pm) with a display of regional costumes, carpets, weaponry, metalwork and jewellery.

On the way back to the Place des Ferblantiers is the wonderful **Dar Tiskiwin** (open daily 9.30am–12.30pm and 3.30–5.30pm) which takes visitors on a journey from Marrakesh to Timbuktu looking at the Dutch anthropologist Bert Flint's amazing collection of crafts and textiles.

Garden City

Marrakesh is a blooming desert oasis with many gardens open to the public. South of the medina lies the **Agdal Garden**, a vast royal pleasure garden of olives groves, fruit orchards and huge pools of water. Other gardens in the city include the Menara (near the airport) and the exotic **Jardin Majorelle**, a botanical garden created in the 1920s by the French artist Jacques Majorelle and restored by fashion designer Yves Saint Laurent.

The newest garden in town, and a perfect place to cool down after the Jemaa el Fna is the **Cyber Park Moulay Abdel Salam**, an 18th-century garden beautifully restored by the Foundation Mohammed VI for the Protection of the Environment in conjunction with Maroc Télécom, with a cyber café as its centre.

Monday market at Tnine Ourika in the Ourika Valley

Day Trips from Marrakesh

If you want to escape the heat of Marrakesh, the **Ourika Valley**, with its olive and almond groves, offers welcome relief. The P2017 from Marrakesh weaves its way up the valley alongside the Ourika River, coming to an abrupt halt at Setti Fatma. There are pretty eateries and swimming pools along the way and pleasant walks to surrounding waterfalls. Off this road, 10km (6 miles) before Setti Fatma, is the 30-km (19-mile) road to **Oukaïmeden**, North Africa's highest ski resort. There are pistes for all abilities, and equipment can be hired in the village. There is normally snow from December to April. In summer there are hiking options using Oukaïmeden as a base.

Two and a half hours east of Marrakesh lie the spectacular **Ouzoud Falls**, where three tiers of water cascade 100 metres (330 ft) into a verdant gorge below. There are basic restaurants overlooking the falls and a few simple hotels nearby.

The village of Aït Arbi above the Dadès Gorge, High Atlas

THE HIGH ATLAS AND ATLANTIC COAST

Marrakesh is the starting point for trips throughout southern Morocco, in particular to Essaouira on the Atlantic coast, and, to the southeast, Ouarzazate on the far side of the Atlas Mountains. From the latter, routes lead east along the Atlas or south via the Draa Valley to the desert. You can travel directly to Essaouira by car, CTM bus or slower local buses in two and a half to four hours, on a main road through gently rolling farmland.

The **Tizi n'Test** (may be closed in winter) is a dramatic route through the Atlas Mountains from Marrakesh to the walled city of Taroudannt. Without stops, the 222km (138 miles) takes about five hours, passing **Berber villages**, kasbahs and fine landscapes. Take Route R203 south from Marrakesh past **Asni**, a Berber village with a lively Saturday market. A side road links Asni to **Imlil**, a good centre for walking and trekking and the base for climbing **Mount Toubkal**, at 4,167 metres (13,670ft) the highest peak in the Atlas. The stunning **Kasbah du Toubkal** (<www.kasbahdu toubkal.com>) just outside Imlil is a perfect stop for lunch or a base for trekking. About 2km (1 mile) south of Imlil is Aremd, gateway to the **Toubkal National Park**.

Approximately 11km (7 miles) beyond Asni on the Route R203 is **Marigha**, a good base for exploring. Two restaurants here make good lunch stops: La Bergerie, a Provençal-style guesthouse set in rambling gardens, and L'Oliveraie de Marigha, where you can eat a light lunch and have a swim.

Beyond Marigha, about 10km (6 miles) past the village of Ijoujak, a paved road on the right leads to the beautiful, semi-ruined 12th-century **Tin Mal Mosque**, birthplace of the Almohad movement that gave rise to the Berber dynasty. Superbly situated, this mosque, roughly contemporary with the Koutoubia in Marrakesh, is one of the few open to non-Muslims (closed Fri).

The **Tizi n'Test Pass**, which reaches a height of 2,092 metres (6,860ft) above sea level, offers fabulous views of the region, but be warned that the way through the pass entails a lengthy series of hairpin bends. At the summit of the pass a small restaurant has panoramic views southwards across the Souss Valley, with the ridge of the Anti-Atlas Mountains rising majestically above the haze.

On the far side of the pass the road descends to join Highway N10. From the junction it is an easy drive to the city of Taroudannt.

Titan Atlas

Inspired by Greek myth, Europeans named the mountain range Atlas. According to the legend, after Titan Atlas was turned to stone by Perseus, he became a mountain supporting the heavens. Bowed by the weight, Atlas genuflected towards the setting sun in northwest Africa.

Taroudannt

The walled city of **Taroudannt**, 225km (140 miles) from Marrakesh, is one of Morocco's more easy-going destinations. Surrounded by olive groves, citrus orchards and green fields, watered with the melting snows of the High Atlas, it is at the commercial hub of the Souss Valley. At a time when all coastal towns were open to naval attack, Taroudannt's inland location and high walls made it the natural choice as the region's capital. Its impressive fortifications, built by the Saadians in the 16th century and in good repair, are the town's most striking attraction. Within the walls, the dusty squares and shady souks offer great shopping opportunities for carpets, leather goods and Berber jewellery.

Salesman on the Tizi n'Tichka

The 19th-century palace in the kasbah is now a hotel, the Palais Salam *(see page 136)*, with comfortable rooms around several intimate courtyards.

Ouarzazate

The N9, linking Marrakesh with Ouarzazate, is the highest, most spectacular paved mountain pass in Morocco. The **Tizi n'Tichka Pass**, which reaches 2,260m (7,400ft), snakes through the verdant foothills and *pisé* (rammed earth) villages of the High Atlas, before a series of hairpin bends takes you to Café Tichka – marking the summit of the pass. The landscape then changes, with arid peaks, rocky out-crops and *ksour* (fortified villages) filling the pre-Saharan landscape.

Some 3km (2 miles) after the café a sharp left turn (signposted) takes you the 20km (12 miles) to the ru-ined Glaoui kasbah of **Telouet**. As with many of the kasbahs of the south, it is a crumbling, picturesque relic of the past.

Telouet

Rejoining the main road, it's about an hour to Ouarzazate. Before the turn off to Aït Benhaddou, at Tisseldi Ighrem N'Oudal is the delightful guesthouse of I Rocha (<www.irocha.com>), a good base to explore the region or to stop for lunch (call ahead). **Aït Ben-haddou**, off the main road, 30km/19 miles before Ouarza-zate, is a well-preserved 11th-century *ksar* made famous as the backdrop in films such as *The Sheltering Sky* and *Glad-iator*. The cinema industry continues to bring prosperity here.

Ouarzazate itself is a modern town with a good range of hotels to suit all budgets, but few sights of particular inter-est apart from the beautiful, semi-ruined kasbah of **Taourirt** (open daily 8am–6pm) and its adjoining *ksar*, situated at the end of Avenue Mohammed V. Opposite the kasbah is the **Ensemble Artisanal** (open daily 9am–noon and 2.30–6pm), with stalls selling the region's crafts at fixed prices. Around 5km (3 miles) out of town, another striking kasbah at **Tiffoultoute** (8am–7pm) has been converted into a restau-rant that caters mainly to tour groups.

The Draa Valley

The highway south from Ouarzazate leads across barren and rocky plains, climbs over a pass and descends through spectacular stratified rock scenery to the oasis town of **Agdz**, the region's administrative centre. In the distance the peak of Djebel Kissane rises like a massive Bedouin tent.

Here the road joins the **Draa Valley**, a wide green swathe of date palms and pink mud villages squeezed between great scarps of naked yellow rock. The Draa is Morocco's longest river, but only after very heavy rains does it flow all the way from its source in the Atlas to its mouth on the Atlantic coast, near Tan Tan.

Roadside gems

Roadside stalls sell fine ammonites, rocks packed with crystals, and semi-precious stones such as amethysts and quartz. Mostly, gems are genuine, but be cautious.

South of Agdz, the road follows the river past fortified villages *(ksour)* built as protection against raids by Saharan nomads. A turn-off left leads to the impressive **Tamnougalt** *ksar*. Back on the main road, 8km (5 miles) further south on the other side of the river, is the kasbah of **Timiderte**, isolated like a medieval fortress, and a classic image of the southern Draa. Later you come to **Tinzouline**, where there is a prehistoric site with remarkable Iron Age rock paintings of animals.

The valley narrows to a rocky defile for a short way before reaching the oasis town of **Zagora**, 164km (105 miles) from Ouarzazate. With good hotels, Zagora is a springboard for trips into the desert and palmeries of the Sahara. The black volcanic Mount Zagora dominates the town. From here, the road continues for 98km (61 miles), passing oases and *ksour*, to **M'Hamid**, a frontier post bordering the Sahara, where nomads gather for the Monday market. To arrange jeep or camel desert excursions ask at the Sahara Services office (<www.saharaservices.info>) or at any hotel.

The Dadès Valley to the Desert

A good road leads east from Ouarzazate along the broad **Dadès Valley**, with the slopes of the High Atlas on the left and the jagged peaks of the Anti-Atlas to the right. After 30km (19 miles) is the dense palmery of the **Skoura** oasis, where there are several good accommodation options. At Boumalne, turn left on a minor road that leads to the village of Msemrir. (Buses or taxi rides are available from Msemrir.)

The road passes through the fabulous scenery of the **Dadès Gorge**, where the near-vertical rock strata have been eroded into fins and razorback ridges of red, green and ochre. Beyond the splendid kasbah at **Aït Arbi** the river disappears into a narrow gorge, and the road switchbacks over a ridge to the upper valley. Almond and walnut trees and cultivated fields spread beneath villages of *pisé* (rammed earth) houses. After 25km (15 miles) the valley narrows to a gorge. To

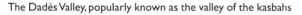

The Dadès Valley, popularly known as the valley of the kasbahs

The village of Merzouga at the base of the Erg Chebbi dunes

continue beyond Msemrir into the mountains and descend into the Todra Gorge you need a four-wheel-drive vehicle.

Beyond Boumalne the main road climbs on to a barren plateau, where sun has burnished the rocks to an iridescent bronze, then descends to the administrative centre of **Tinerhir**, with plenty of hotels and restaurants. On the far side of town a road leads through a luxuriant palmery, and after some 15km (9 miles) reaches the mouth of the **Todra Gorge**. This magnificent limestone ravine is less beautiful but more impressive than that at Dadès, being 300m (985ft) deep but only 10m (32 ft) wide at its narrowest point.

Three hours south-east of Tinerhir are the colossal Saharan dunes of **Erg Chebbi**. A walk or camel ride at sunrise or sunset across them is Morocco's most impressive desert experience. A 60-km (40-mile) road (mostly tarmac) from Erfoud takes you to **Merzouga** (the village just before the dunes), where you will find a cluster of basic hotels.

Agadir

Though named after a 16th-century fortress *(agadir)* on a hill-top to its north, **Agadir**, 70km (43 miles) west of Taroudan-nt, is brand new. An earthquake in 1960 levelled the old town, killing 15,000 people and leaving 50,000 homeless.

A new city was built as a resort around the sandy bay here. Modern architecture, wide, tree-lined avenues, open squares and pedestrian precincts contrast with the narrow streets of a traditional Moroccan town. The focus downtown is the shopping centre of Place du Prince Héritier Sidi Mohammed. Low-rise hotels separate the centre from Agadir's splendid beach, which stretches 10km (6 miles) to the south. Take care when swimming here, as the sea can be rough.

Excursion from Agadir

A highway leads south from Agadir across stony plains dotted with scrub and stunted trees. After about 90km (65 miles) the landscape changes to palm trees and sand as

The Land of the Argan Tree

The country between Agadir and Essaouira is commonly known as 'The Land of the Argan Tree'. A relative of the olive, the argan is a twisted, tortured-looking tree endemic to this region. Goats have become adept at climbing into its branches to eat the fruits.

Argan oil is made from the nut and adds a great nutty flavour to salad dressings and *tajines*. Berbers believe the oil keeps them healthy well into their old age; it is proven to reduce cholesterol and is also used in cosmetics. Produced by the Berber women in the region, it takes 30kg (66lbs) of nuts and 15 hours to extract 1 litre of oil. People sell argan oil on the roadside, but it is advisable to buy it from a shop or a cooperative like Cooperative Amal (tel: 024 78 81 41; <www. targanine. com>) in Tamanar, 80km (50 miles) north of Agadir.

Tiznit comes into view. Protected by a massive, crenellated wall, Tiznit has little to offer tourists, but the jewellers' souk is a good source of old Berber brooches and pins. The coast at Aglou-Plage, 17km (10 miles) west of town, has a fine surf beach, and further down lies the charming coastal village of **Mirleft**.

A scenic four-hour 110-km (68-mile) drive inland from Tiznit leads to the mountain village of **Tafraoute**, which offers many options for keen walkers and mountain-bikers (bikes can be rented in town). But Tafraoute is best known for **Les Roches Bleues**, huge boulders painted blue in 1984 by the Belgian artist Jean Verame; he wanted his giant work of art to give new meaning to the term 'landscape painting'.

Continuing south from Tiznit, you reach **Goulimine**, 200km (124 miles) from Agadir and at the very edge of the Sahara. Until the 1930s the town's Saturday camel market was the biggest in the Western Sahara. Now there are few camels and the market deals in other local goods. Goulimine has several eating places, shops and an old *ksar*. In June the *moussem* (festival) of Sidi M'Hamed Benamar *(see page 98)* attracts a large number of desert tribesmen, the 'Blue Men', nomads whose skin takes on a blue colour from the indigo dye in their robes.

Essaouira

Situated equidistant from Marrakesh and Agadir (175km/110 miles from each), the walled Atlantic port of **Essaouira** was known as Mogador in ancient times. The purple dye extracted here from local shellfish was used to create the 'imperial purple' that was heavily in demand in 1st-century Rome.

The town you see today is only 200 years old. Sultan Mohammed ibn Abdallah built a military port, and a French architect prisoner of his designed the town plan, so the streets are laid out in a more orderly pattern than those in most Moroccan medinas. Since it is often subject to strong Atlantic winds, Essaouira has not been greatly developed for mass tourism. But the attractive beach, which stretches way to the south and is lined with hotels and restaurants, draws year-round European wind-surfers.

At the town end of the beach is the fishing and boat-building harbour. Near the port, from lunchtime through to dinner, fishermen cook up freshly caught fish and serve them at picnic tables at reasonable prices – you can choose your fish directly from the catch. The **Skala de la Ville** is a cannon battery that formed part of the port's defences and has an impressive circular North Bastion. The battery offers good views over the town walls and sea.

Essaouira

The Rue de la Skala leads past souvenir stalls to the little town square, Place Prince Moulay el Hassan, where there is a selection of attractive café-restaurants. Off to the right is the main street, lined with tidy shops and little souks famed for the carpenters' workshops, located under the ramparts, where craftsmen produce handsome thuya wood furniture.

Essaouira's week-long annual Gnaoua music festival in June attracts tens of thousands of Moroccan and foreign tourists.

WHAT TO DO

The rich variety of Morocco's arts and crafts, and the souks in which they are sold, are among the country's greatest attractions, while its beaches, mountains and deserts are ideal for sporting activities. The numerous festivals and national events are also worth a detour.

SHOPPING

Every town and village has its souk, no matter how small: cities such as Fez and Marrakesh have entire districts crammed with souks, each one dedicated to a particular trade, while country villages have a weekly general market.

Bargaining

Bargaining is a way of life in Morocco and, although it's difficult for Westerners to live in a world without price tags, you need to play the game to avoid paying over the odds.

Here are a few suggestions to help your dealings. In Morocco, bargaining is social interaction: keep a sense of humour, always be polite (so that you can return to a shop if an item you like really cannot be found at a better price elsewhere) and, if you are really interested in buying, accept mint tea if it is offered – it enhances the friendly, slow nature of the bargaining. It never hurts to ask casually in

Provincial souks

Souks are not just to be found in the main cities. During your stay be sure to visit at least one of the following: Agadir on Sunday, Taroudannt on Thursday and Sunday, Ifrane on Sunday, Tinerhir on Monday, Moulay Idriss on Saturday, Zagora on Wednesday and Sunday, Ouarzazate on Sunday, or Tafraoute, held on Wednesday.

a few shops about the opening price of an item you might consider buying, even if it isn't exactly the one you want. No two items are identical, but when you find the painted mirror or kelim rug that you really like and ask the opening price, you will at least have some idea of parameters.

Never begin the bargaining process unless you find something you really want to purchase, and never show that you are in love with an item – always appear hesitant: 'It's not exactly what I'm looking for, but about how much is this?' You do not have to raise your offer in response to each price reduction by a merchant. It never hurts to decline and politely try to leave: 'I'm sorry, I just don't think I can pay more and my husband isn't feeling well, we've really got to go.' Merchants hate to let an interested customer get away. Never tell a merchant your maximum price: this will then become a minimum for him.

Morocco is filled with beautiful things that would cost far more if you could find them in your home country. Remember, even if a shop in a souk claims to be a 'cooperative' and have 'fixed prices', this may not be true. A good final price really depends on how much the merchant needs to convert some of his stock to ready cash.

Fixed prices

If you prefer not to bargain for your purchases, visit the local Ensemble Artisanal, a state-run organisation of crafts shops in major destinations that has fixed prices (ask at the tourist office for the nearest one). Here you can gain some idea of the range of crafts available and the prices you can expect to pay (the variety will be greater and the final prices a little lower in the souks).

What to Buy

Architectural details. Carved panels, doors and windows from elegant mansions and primitive Sahara villages are increasingly popular and can be shipped.

Leather slippers, known as *babouches*

Carpets and rugs. Moroccan carpets generally have a deeper pile and a looser weave of larger knots than the more familiar Persian or Turkish ones. The finest and most expensive are those from Rabat; tribal *kelims* (flat-weave rugs) are considered by many to be the country's real forté. Although beautiful, Moroccan knotted and kelim rugs are not durable, and are best used as wall hangings, divan or bed covers, or on floors that don't receive heavy traffic. Traditionally, kelims were hung in tents or farmhouses as room dividers; the sequins sometimes sewn onto these kelims helped to reflect and disperse candlelight. There is a wide range of regional designs. Smaller shops in Marrakesh, Fez and Meknes, and the Tuesday carpet market at Khimesset, between Rabat and Meknes, are good places to find older and high-quality pieces.

Inlaid bone boxes and mirror frames. Beautiful, but check for odour; if the bone is not properly cleaned and cured, the item will reek and the inlay will buckle.

Fresh herbs for sale

Jewellery. Berber jewellery made of silver, amber, and semi-precious stones is strikingly beautiful and can be found at a fraction of the price you would pay back home. Look for old, one-of-a-kind hand-engraved designs, especially Hands of Fatima, believed to ward off the evil eye. Shops in Taroudannt and Tiznit as well as Essaouira and Marrakesh have good supplies.

Leather. Ultra-soft, fine-grained Morocco leather is made from goatskin and is used for book bindings, desk sets, portfolios, wallets, gloves and many other articles. Fez is top of this field. Leather jackets, suitcases, satchels and handbags are also popular. Leather clothing can be made to order in Agadir. Another favourite buy is a pair of traditional backless leather slippers, or *babouches*: yellow or beige are popular choices for men, and red for women.

Metalwork. Look for copper or brass trays with fine, ornate hammered designs, which, along with a small folding wooden stand, make attractive tables. Wrought-iron lanterns, mirror frames, tables with tiny hand-carved *zellige*-tile inlaid tops, and even custom-made, contemporary designer furniture are in good supply in Marrakesh in the iron-workers' souk near Medersa Ben Youssef.

Pottery. Fez, Meknes, Sale, Safi and Marrakesh are the best places to look for quality pottery. The classic souvenir is a conical *tajine* dish, but the choice of articles available is wide, and ranges from hand-painted plates to beautiful antique bowls and vases. Rough pottery bowls from the Atlas and Rif Mountains, usually dusty beige, are interesting objets of primitive design.

Spices and herbs. Abundant heaps of fresh herbs and spices are on sale in the souks. Saffron is very cheap by Western standards; olives, nuts and argan oil are also good buys.

Woodwork. Essaouira is famous for boxes and turned containers of thuya, a lavishly grained, aromatic wood that grows only on the Essaouira stretch of the Atlantic coast; thuya is also made into chessboards, inlaid tables, backgammon sets and sculpture. Thuya pieces of lesser quality are available throughout Morocco. Elaborately painted wood is also a Moroccan tradition: look for ornate painted mirror frames and hanging wall shelves of all sizes. Antique boxes and chests with carved arabesque motifs and chairs and tables made from sweet-smelling cedar wood can be found in the souks of major cities.

Pottery designs

ACTIVE PURSUITS

Swimming and water sports. Morocco has 2,000km (1,250 miles) of coastline facing the Atlantic Ocean, with several outstanding **beaches**. The best are at Agadir and Essaouira, and at Asilah, south of Tangier. Do not venture out of your depth anywhere on the Atlantic coast: the undertow can sweep you out to sea in a matter of minutes.

Morocco's Mediterranean beaches, however, are pleasant and varied, and generally free from the threat of undertow. The resorts backed by the Rif Mountains are very attractive, most notably those around Al Hoceima. Explore the possibilities at Cabo Negro, Smir-Restinga and Taïfor.

Surfing, wind-surfing and kite-surfing are extremely popular on the breezy Atlantic coast of Morocco. Tarhazoute, north of Agadir, and Essaouira have international reputations as two of Morocco's best sites. In the UK, packages are available with the excellent Surf Maroc (tel: 01794 322 709, <www.surfmaroc.co.uk>).

Sailing and scuba-diving. Both are available in Agadir.

Fishing. The Atlantic and Mediterranean coasts provide opportunities for deep-sea angling and rock-fishing as well as surf-casting, while the waters of the Atlas are rich in trout, bass and pike. Freshwater anglers require a permit from the Service des Eaux et Forêts (Waters and Forests Service), which also gives out information on closed seasons and local regulations. Contact the ONMT for details *(see page 126).*

A round of golf in Marrakesh

On horseback through the Atlas

Golf. The **Royal Dar-Es-Salam Club** at Rabat has one 9-hole and two 18-hole championship golf courses, designed by Robert Trent Jones, with luxurious clubhouse facilities. There are other 18-hole courses at Mohammedia, Tangier, El Jadida and Marrakesh, and 9-hole courses at Cabo Negro (near Tetouan), Meknes, Fez, Casablanca and Ouarzazate. Courses are open all year, and green fees are comparable to those in Europe. Marrakesh's Palmeraie Golf Palace Hotel *(see page 133)*, next to the 18-hole Robert Trent Jones course, is geared to golf holidays.

Horse-riding. You can hire a horse in Agadir for a beach or countryside ride. Treks into the High Atlas are run from the Hôtel La Roseraie at Ouirgane, near Marrakesh. For further information, contact the ONMT *(see page 126)*.

Hunting. There is a 190-sq. km (73-sq. mile) hunting reserve at Arbaoua, near the coast south of Larache; smaller reserves are near Marrakesh, Agadir, Kabila and Benslimane. Book through a specialist tour operator in your home country or contact the ONMT *(see page 126)*.

Winter sports. You can ski in the Atlas Mountains between December and April, snow conditions permitting. The biggest resort is Oukaimeden, 70km (44 miles) south of Marrakesh, at an altitude of 3,200m (10,500ft); it has a few hotels, one chair-lift and six tows, and equipment rental is available. There are smaller ski areas at Michliffen, near Azrou.

Trekking and mountain biking. Several adventure holiday companies arrange trekking and mountain-biking trips in the Atlas. The High Atlas in particular offers a good range of high-level, multi-day walking routes, with accommodation in French Alpine Club mountain huts. It is also possible to travel simply, with a guide and a pack donkey. In winter, the high peaks provide a challenge for experienced mountaineers. The unsurfaced roads and tracks that wind through the valleys are ideal terrain for mountain bikers. Tour companies organise accommodation and Land Rover back-up. To find out more, contact the ONMT *(see page 126)*.

Desert trips. These can be arranged from M'hamid on the edge of the Sahara to the south of Zagora. Camel treks of various lengths and durations can be arranged through local operators (tents are provided for overnight stays), and 4x4 expeditions to the high dunes are also very popular. Camel treks are also available from Merzouga to the southeast of Erfoud, into the dramatic dunes of the Erg Chebbi. Again, tents for overnight stays under the stars are provided.

Walking across the Erg Chebbi

Camels and their drivers in the Dadès Valley

Rafting and kayaking. Good rafting is to be had on the Dadès and Ahenssal rivers. Remember than when snow melts or rains fall the rivers of the High and Middle Atlas quickly swell; never take unnecessary risks. For details of watersport tour companies, contact the ONMT *(see page 126)*.

ENTERTAINMENT

Early evening is promenade time in all Moroccan towns, when it seems as if the entire population turns out for a stroll along the main avenue with family and friends and a chat over coffee or mint tea.

Nightlife

Major hotels and traditional Moroccan restaurants in the main tourist cities offer evening entertainment in the form of a Moroccan banquet, with folk music, dancing and, perhaps,

Evening in an elegant palace

a belly dancer. Some of the expensive medina restaurants in Fez and Marrakesh are in converted former palaces, wonderful for an extravagant, leisurely meal and worth visiting for the decor alone. Although not as cheap as it once was, a banquet in a palace represents a reasonably priced evening out compared to dinner in European cities.

In Rabat, Casablanca, Marrakesh, Tangier and Agadir, you'll find a few European-style bars and discos. They stay open until late – ask your hotel receptionist for a recommendation. There is a casino in Marrakesh's Hotel Mamounia, but be sure to dress smartly or you won't be admitted.

Folklore and Festivals

The best possible way to experience genuine Moroccan folk music and dance, away from a tourist-oriented environment, is to attend one of the **moussems**, or religious festivals, held in honour of a local saint or holy man *(marabout)*. People from far and wide converge on the saint's tomb for several days of festivities. There are hundreds of annual *moussems* in Morocco, ranging from small local gatherings to national holidays. Many are held during the months of August and September, following the harvest. You can ask locally whether any are taking place during your stay; the most important ones are listed on page 98 of this guide.

Folk dancing is a major part of any popular festival or religious holiday. The most unusual is the *guedra* dance, performed by Berber women from the extreme south – heavily veiled dancers perform in a kneeling position (the dance was originally performed in low desert tents) and entrance their audience with undulating movements of the arms and hands.

Mystical **Gnaoua** music was introduced to Morocco by slaves brought here from sub-Saharan Africa by Arab traders. You can recognise Gnaoua dancers by their black-and-white costumes decorated with cowrie shells (also common in West Africa) and by the quick and exciting beat of their drums and metal 'castanets' called *garagab*.

The *fantasia* is the most exciting of all Moroccan traditions, a breathtaking display of horsemanship. Charging horsemen perform daring manoeuvres and acrobatics, sometimes to the accompaniment of gunfire. *Fantasias* are offered at most large festivals and at major tourist destinations. It is an experience not to be missed. Ask at your hotel or the ONMT *(see page 126)* if one is taking place during your stay.

Gnaoua performers

Calendar of Events

To experience genuine Moroccan folklore, attend one of the many *moussems* (religious restivals) held in honour of a local saint or *marabout* (holy man). Exact dates should be confirmed at local tourist offices.

February Almond Blossom Festival in Tafraoute, southeast of Agadir.

March Marathon des Sables (Desert Marathon).

Early May Moussem of Zaou'a el Kettania, Essaouira.

May–June Rose Petal Festival, El Kelaa M'Gounna (near Ouarzazate).

National Folklore Festival, Marrakesh.

International Festival of Sacred Music, Fez.

Festival at Salé, in honour of *marabout* Sidi Abdallah Ben Hassan.

Moussem of Sidi Mohammed Ma el-Aineen (Atlantic coast)

June Moussem of Sidi Moussa, Casablanca.

Moussem of Sidi M'Hamed Benamar, Goulimine.

Festival of Cherries, Sefrou.

Popular Arts Festival, Marrakesh.

Gnaoua Music Festival, Essaouira.

July International Music Festival, Asilah.

Moussem of Outa Hammou, Chaouen.

Moussem of Moulay Abdallah, El-Jadida.

August Moussem of Sidi Lahcen, Temara (coastal shrine near Rabat).

International Arts Festival, Asilah.

Moussem of Dar Zhirou, Rabat.

Moussem of Sitti Fatma, Ourika Valley (near Marrakesh).

Moussem of Sidi Mogdoul, Essaouira, late in the month.

September Moussem of Moulay Idriss II, Fez.

Moussem of Sidi Abdalhak ben Yasin, Marrakesh.

Moussem of El Guern, Marrakesh.

Moussem of Moulay Idriss, Moulay Idriss (near Meknes).

National Fantasia Festival, Meknes.

October Art and folklore festival, Agadir.

November Date festival, Erfoud.

December International Film Festival, Marrakesh

EATING OUT

Morocco has one of the most exciting and exotic cuisines in the world, influenced by the cooking of the Berbers, the Middle East, Andalusia and France. The bazaars and markets are filled with stalls selling fresh breads, preserved olives, dried fruits stuffed with nuts, and savoury semolina cakes that you can take away and eat on the hoof. Wonderful hole-in-the-wall establishments offer soups, baked dishes, freshly fried fish and barbecued kebabs. The new cities *(villes nouvelles)* offer a good variety of competent Moroccan and international restaurants with an occasional pizzeria or Vietnamese/Chinese place to round out the choices. Cafés are a Moroccan interpretation of the French variety, with lots of open-air seating where you can linger for hours over tea or coffee.

Place settings

It is well worth experiencing the richness of Moroccan cooking in one of the lavish former palaces and great houses of Fez, Marrakesh, and Rabat that have been turned into restaurants. Most of the good **palace restaurants** serve three- to seven-course meals, and, for most, a reservation is needed, especially if you plan to order dishes that involve many hours of preparation. Your meal may be accompanied by musicians, folk dancers or a belly dancer.

A Moroccan Feast

A full Moroccan feast contains examples of the kinds of dishes you'll encounter as you travel across the country. The first course is generally a selection of intricate salads, including finely chopped tomatoes, onions and cucumbers with parsley; a hearty purée of smoked, garlic-saturated aubergines; cooked tomatoes in seasoned honey; marinated carrots; lentils and onion; and *briouats*, small, lightly fried pastry envelopes filled with spiced meat, vegetables or fish. Alternatively, you may begin with *harira*, a lamb and chick-pea soup, served to rich and poor alike and traditionally used to break the daily fast during the holy month of Ramadan. A good *harira* is full of flavours (including lemon and coriander) and

Cooks in action on Jemaa el Fna in Marrakesh

can contain rice, pasta, boiled egg and even dates. Next comes the *mechoui* – a succulent whole lamb, slowly spit-roasted (during festivals in the countryside, and at some rustic restaurants, you may see whole lambs being roasted over outdoor fires).

Ramadan

Although non-Muslims are not obliged to fast during Ramadan, it is considered a general courtesy to refrain from eating or drinking in public.

At this point, you might be ready to pack it in, but the next course may be *pastilla*, regarded by many as the jewel in the crown of Moroccan gastronomy. It is made of layers of paper-thin *ouarka* (flaky filo-like pastry) interspersed with pigeon or chicken meat, ground almonds, saffron, eggs and spices dusted with cinnamon, all covered with powdered sugar. Some say the number of layers is a good clue to the *pastilla's* quality. You can find basic *pastillas* on the street, but those served at a good quality restaurant (or in the home) are far superior.

Pastilla could be dessert for all its delicacy and sweetness, but an interesting *tajine* (stew) is usually offered as the next course. Named after the earthenware vessel with a conical cover in which it is served, the *tajine* might be slowly simmered beef with prunes and almonds, or lamb with raisins and sweet onions, or chicken with preserved lemon and olives, or fish stuffed with tomatoes, onions, potatoes, coriander, dill and other herbs. Traditionally, a *tajine* was cooked by burying the pot in a charcoal fire in the ground.

A mound of fluffy couscous, or steamed semolina, the staple grain of Morocco, is the *pièce de résistance* of the meal, covering a colourful assortment of stewed vegetables or pieces of succulent lamb. Couscous is served at the tables of the richest and poorest homes in Morocco, traditionally on Friday, and although, to the uninitiated, one mound of couscous may seem much like any other, there are many ways to prepare the grain.

The earthenware *tajine* has a distinctive conical lid

Then come the Moroccan pastries, including the traditional *cornes de gazelle*, heavy pastry crescents stuffed with ground nuts and cinnamon. Finally there is a platter of assorted fruits, followed by a glass of mint tea or a cup of thick, strong, Moroccan coffee. If you don't like your mint tea very sweet (the way most Moroccans drink it), ask for it with *shwiyeh sukar* (a little sugar).

Other Specialities

Kefta are meatballs of minced lamb flavoured with cumin and coriander, cooked on charcoal. *Merguez* is a spicy North African beef or lamb sausage. *Rgha'ifs* are fried pancakes, folded and stuffed with a variety of fillings, served hot.

Vegetarian Dishes

Moroccan salads, both cold and hot, as well as breads, olives and omelettes are always good choices. You can ask for couscous *sans viande* (without meat), although more often than not, the vegetables in the couscous are cooked in meat stock.

Fish and Seafood

The country's long coastline and numerous lakes and streams provide a rich catch of fish for the Moroccan table. Red mullet, dorado, sardines, sea bass and Atlas trout head the list. Fish can be used in a *tajine* or couscous but is more often grilled or poached and served alone as a main course. Moroccan waters also yield a fine selection of *fruits de mer* (seafood) – especially *poulpe* (octopus) and *calamar* (squid), usually served deep-fried in a light batter. A popular delicacy is *elvers* (or *civelles*), baby eels the size of matchsticks, sautéed in butter and garlic and served with bread. The coastal resort of Oualidia is famous for its superb oysters.

Liquid Refreshment

Although the consumption of alcohol is forbidden by Islamic law, wine, beer and spirits are available freely to visitors in the hotels, bars and restaurants of the *villes nouvelles* and coastal resorts. Moroccan wines are well worth trying *(see page 50)*. Even modest restaurants will have a few good local wines to choose from, and the better places will have a varied selection. The home-brewed beers, Flag and Casablanca, are light, continental-tasting and cheaper than imported brands.

Tea service

Mint tea *(thé à la menthe)*, a sweetened infusion of mint leaves and green or black tea, is the most common refreshment *(see page 10)*. Other drinks include coffee (usually *café au lait* or Turkish), fruit juices and milkshakes. Mineral water *(eau minérale)*, either sparkling *(gazeuse)* or still *(non-gazeuse)*, is available in all restaurants and groceries. Most non-alcoholic drinks are moderately priced, but imported wines and spirits are expensive.

To Help You Order…

I'd like a/an/some…   **J'aimerais …**

beer	**une bière**	mineral	**de l'eau**
bread	**du pain**	water	**minérale**
chicken	**du poulet**	fizzy	**gazeuse**
coffee	**un café**	salt	**du sel**
dessert	**un dessert**	pepper	**du poivre**
eggs	**des œufs**	seafood	**des fruits de mer**
fish	**du poisson**	soup	**de la soupe**
fruit	**des fruits**	tea	**du thé**
lamb	**de l'agneau**	(mint)	**(à la menthe)**
meat	**de la viande**	vegetables	**des légumes**
milk	**du lait**	wine	**du vin**

…and Read the Menu

Moroccan staples include couscous, *harira*, *pastilla*, *tajines*, *kefta* and *merguez (see descriptions pages 100–3)* as well as:

brochette	meat kebab	**hout**	fish
djej	chicken	**khobz**	bread

Sensational Snacks

The Moroccan pleasure in food is reflected in the array of snacks sold by street vendors. These include cactus fruit, freshly roasted chickpeas, or snails in a cumin-flavoured liquor ladled out of a vat. You'll also find *tortilla*, freshly fried potato crisps sprinkled with sea salt, and fresh fried sugared doughnuts *(sfen)*.

Dining etiquette

In Morocco, as in all Muslim countries, it is the custom not to eat with your left hand – nor should you use it when greeting anyone.

HANDY TRAVEL TIPS

An A–Z Summary of Practical Information

A

ACCOMMODATION *(logement, hôtels;* see CAMPING, YOUTH HOSTELS and the list of RECOMMENDED HOTELS starting on page 128)

Hotels in all price categories in Morocco are usually less expensive than in Europe and the US. Accommodation ranges from very cheap, unclassified hotels to luxury, five-star international establishments. The former offer only basic facilities – smelly toilets, sagging mattresses, and no towels or hot water. If you want European levels of comfort and service, then choose at least a three-star hotel.

Well-run, often very luxurious hotels have sprung up in mansions and palaces in the medinas of several cities. Greatly in demand, they range from simple to plush; in exchange for atmosphere and charm, you sometimes give up some standard hotel elements. We've listed some of the best in our RECOMMENDED HOTELS section.

By law, prices must be displayed in reception and in the rooms. The quoted rates usually include VAT (TVA in French), but other local taxes – Taxe Promotion Touristique (TPT) and Taxe de Séjour (TS) – may add another 5–12dh per night to your bill. Check also whether breakfast is included. Book ahead during the peak periods of July–August, Christmas–New Year and Easter.

Do you have a single/double room?	**Avez-vous une chambre pour une/deux personnes?**
What's the rate per night?	**Quel est le prix pour une nuit?**

AIRPORTS *(aéroports)*

Morocco's main international airports are in Casablanca, Tangier, Agadir and Marrakesh. **Casablanca** is served by Mohammed V Airport (tel: 022 53 90 40), 30km (18 miles) south of the city. There is a rail link between the airport and central Casablanca (35dh), with connections to Rabat; trains run hourly 8.30am–10.30pm, and take 20 minutes to Casablanca-Voyageurs station or 30 minutes to Casablanca-Port (more convenient for the city centre). A shuttle-bus runs between the airport and the CTM bus station downtown (hourly services 6am–11pm; journey time 40 minutes). *Grands taxis (see page 123)* are also available for about 200–250dh.

Agadir is served by Al Massira airport (tel: 028 83 91 12), situated 25km (15 miles) east of the resort. Package holiday-makers on charter flights are met by bus for the 30-minute trip into town. Independent travellers must take a *grand taxi* (about 150–180dh for up to 6 passengers); to cut costs share with other travellers (arrange a group before approaching a driver).

Tangier airport, Boukhalef Souahel (tel: 039 39 37 20), is 15km (9 miles) southwest of the city. If you are not on a charter flight, which is usually met by a bus, you will have to take a taxi. A *grand taxi* costs about 100dh: to share the cost with other travellers, arrange a group inside the airport and agree the fare with the driver before getting in.

Marrakesh airport (tel: 024 44 78 65) is about 5km (3 miles) southwest of the city. A taxi to town is around 80–100dh.

B

BICYCLE/MOPED HIRE *(location de vélos/motos)*

Marrakesh is flat, making it an ideal place for cycling. You can hire bicycles at the Hotel Foucauld and Hotel Ali, near Jemaa el Fna, in the Hivernage (outside the Hotel Andaluz) or from Action Sports Loisirs (Apt 4, 1 Avenue Yacoub el-Mansour, Guéliz, tel: 024 43 09 31), who also organise cycle tours. Bicycles and mopeds can be hired at hotels in Agadir, Taroudannt, Ouarzazate and Zagora. Inspect the bike carefully before taking it, as you will have to pay for repairs if it breaks down. Check that the quoted rates for mopeds include tax and insurance. Mopeds and scooters can be dangerous, so go slowly and keep to quiet roads until you get the hang of them.

BUDGETING FOR YOUR TRIP (See also MONEY)

To give you an idea of how to budget once you're there, here is a
list of approximate prices in Moroccan dirhams (dh).

Airport transfer. Casablanca: train 35dh, bus 20dh, taxi 200dh.
Agadir: taxi 150dh. Tangier: taxi 100dh. Marrakesh: taxi 100dh.

Bicycle and moped hire. Rates are negotiable, but average around
70–80dh a day. Motorbikes (125cc) cost from 200dh a day.

Buses. City buses have a flat fare of 3dh. Long-distance coach, one
way: Casablanca–Marrakesh 85dh; Marrakesh–Ouarzazate 80dh.

Entertainment. Nightclub admission (including first drink), 200dh.

Guides. Official guides, hired through the local tourist office, charge
120dh per half-day.

Hotelsv Double room with bath: one-star 300dh, two-star
300–500dh, three-star 500–700dh, four-star from 750dh, five-star
from 1,500dh.

Meals and drinks. Continental breakfast in a four-star hotel 60dh,
set-menu dinner 250dh; in a two-star hotel, breakfast 40dh, set-
menu dinner 150dh. Drinks (at pavement café): soft drinks 10dh,
coffee 8dh, mint tea 6dh, bottle of wine 100dh.

Sightseeing. Admission to museums/historic buildings: 15–30dh.

Taxis. Cross-town trip in a *petit taxi (see page 123)*: about 10–15dh.

Trains. Adult single, second-class: Tangier–Rabat 90dh, Rabat–Fez
76dh, Rabat–Marrakesh 112dh; first-class is about 30 percent more.

Youth hostels. 20–35dh per person per night.

C

CAMPING (le camping)

Campsites can be found in most of the popular tourist areas of Morocco, especially along the Atlantic coast. Facilities vary from very
basic (a patch of bare earth with a toilet block) to shaded, comfortable sites with electricity, showers, laundry, pool, bar and restaurant. Prices are generally low by European standards. A list of

official sites can be obtained from tourist offices *(see page 126)*. Camping anywhere alone is not recommended; however, camping outside official sites is permitted provided that you obtain permission from the landowner. Morocco offers lots of opportunities for wilderness camping which is, effectively, unrestricted.

CAR HIRE *(location de voitures)*

Although expensive by European and North American standards, hiring a car gives you the freedom to travel at your own pace, and to explore places inaccessible by public transport.

All the major car-hire firms operate in the bit cities and tourist resorts; local firms often charge less than the big international chains, but rates vary widely, so shop around. Be wary of any agency recommended by a 'guide': he is bound to be on commission.

The best rates are usually to be had by booking and paying for your car before you leave home, either directly through an international rental company or as part of a fly-drive package deal. Check that the quoted rate includes Collision Damage Waiver, unlimited mileage and tax (currently 20 percent in Morocco), as these can considerably increase the cost.

You must be aged over 21 to rent a car, and you will need to produce a full driver's licence, which you must have held for a minimum of 12 months, your passport and a major credit card – cash deposits are prohibitively large. In addition, non-European drivers may need to produce an International Driver's Licence; check beforehand with your car-rental company. For an additional fee, some rental companies will provide a driver, if you prefer not to drive yourself. (See also DRIVING.)

I'd like to rent a car	**Je voudrais louer une voiture**
now/tomorrow	**tout de suite/demain**
for one day/a week	**pour une journée/une semaine**

CLIMATE AND CLOTHING

A Mediterranean climate with hot, dry summers and mild, rainy winters extends over the northern and central parts of the country, giving way to a semi-arid desert climate south of the Atlas Mountains. May to September is the best time to visit the coastal resorts and the north of the country, with consistent sunshine and high temperatures, though it can be brutally hot in inland cities such as Fez and Meknes.

Winter is the time to explore the deep south – Marrakesh, Ouarzazate and Zagora are all popular winter-sun destinations. Remember that there can be a huge difference in temperature between day and night, so take warm clothes for the evenings.

The chart below shows the average daily maximum temperature, in degrees centigrade, for each month in Tangier (T), Agadir (A) and Marrakesh (M):

	J	F	M	A	M	J	J	A	S	O	N	D
T	15	16	17	19	21	24	26	27	25	22	18	16
A	20	21	23	23	24	26	27	27	27	26	24	21
M	18	20	23	25	29	33	38	37	33	28	23	19

Clothing. From June to September the days are always hot, but evenings can be cool, so take a jacket or sweater. Also pack long-sleeved tops, a sun-hat and sunblock to protect against the sun. During the rest of the year a light jacket and a raincoat or umbrella will come in handy, while a warm coat for desert nights is essential. Modest clothing should be worn when visiting mosques and other Islamic monuments. Topless sunbathing is only permitted in private hotel grounds, not public beaches. (See also WOMEN TRAVELLERS.)

COMPLAINTS (réclamation)

Any complaints should first be made to the management of the establishment involved. If satisfaction is not obtained, ask to be given the complaints book *(livre des réclamations)*; the law requires that all hotels, restaurants and official guides provide one. Usually, a demand for the complaints book will settle the matter; if not, then seek advice from the local tourist office.

To avoid problems, always establish a price in advance, especially when dealing with guides, taxi drivers and porters at stations.

CRIME AND SAFETY (See also EMERGENCIES and POLICE)

The crime rate is low in Morocco, but is rising. Physical assault against foreigners is very rare, and largely confined to those involved with drugs or prostitution. A police clamp-down has dramatically reduced the problem of being approached by unofficial, or so-called 'faux', guides and hustlers. It is illegal to hassle tourists, and, if caught, *faux guides* may be sent to prison. Most Moroccans will give you directions and help if you feel threatened.

Pickpockets are the most serious problem in Morocco; as in all countries, travellers should keep wallets and identification in deep, securely fastened pockets or money-belts. Do not leave valuables in your hotel room or a parked car.

The area of Ketama in the Rif Mountains has a thriving *kif-* (hashish-) growing industry and is best avoided, especially by drivers, who may be forced to stop and buy cannabis resin.

Report any theft or loss immediately to the police in order to comply with your travel insurance. If your passport is lost or stolen, you should inform your consulate as well *(see page 114)*.

CUSTOMS AND ENTRY FORMALITIES

Citizens of the UK, Republic of Ireland, US, Canada, Australia and New Zealand need only a full passport for visits of up to 90 days; the passport must be valid for at least three months after the date you arrive.

Visas are not required for stays of less than 90 days. (Visa regulations change, so check before you travel.)

Currency restrictions. You can take limitess foreign currency into or out of the country, but must declare on entry amounts over the value of 15,000 dh. It is illegal to import or export Moroccan dh.

Customs. EU citizens may take into Morocco a bottle of wine and a bottle of spirits, or two bottles of wine per adult, as well as 200 cigarettes, 50 cigars or 250g (8oz) tobacco.

D

DRIVING

Motorists planning to take their own vehicle into Morocco will need a full driver's licence *(permis de conduire)*, an international motor insurance certificate and Green Card and a vehicle registration document. An official nationality plate must be displayed near the rear number plate, and headlight beams must be adjusted for driving on the right.

The use of seat belts in both front and back seats is obligatory; fines for non-compliance are stiff. A red warning triangle must be carried. Motorcycle riders and their passengers must wear crash helmets. The minimum legal age for driving in Morocco is 18.

Driving conditions. Drive on the right and pass on the left. Speed limits are 120km/h (73mph) on toll roads, 100km/h (60mph) on highways, and 40 or 60km/h (25 or 38mph) in towns and cities. Traffic joining a road from the right has priority, unless signs or markings indicate otherwise. Cars already on a roundabout (traffic circle) must give way to those joining it. One local quirk you should be prepared for is that drivers making a left turn on a two-lane road often move over to the wrong side of the road before turning – this can be rather disconcerting if you are travelling in the opposite direction.

Driving conditions outside the cities are generally good on the main routes, with long, straight stretches and little traffic. Four-lane motorways *(autoroutes)* link Casablanca, Rabat, Kenitra and

Larache, and extend east to Meknes and Fez. Tolls are 15dh or 20dh between major towns. Minor roads are often too narrow for two vehicles. To pass or overtake you need to move on to the gravel shoulder. Always be on the look-out for pedestrians, donkey carts and mopeds, especially at night.

If you plan to wander off the main routes, a reliable road map is essential. Do not attempt unsurfaced minor roads without a four-wheel-drive vehicle and a local guide. Remember, too, that many roads across the Atlas Mountains are blocked by snow in winter.

Most road signs in Morocco use the standard European pictographs; directional signs are usually in French and Arabic. Stop signs are octagonal and often in Arabic only, as are other signs for traffic regulations.

Déviation	Diversion (detour)
Priorité à droite	Yield to traffic from right
Vous n'avez pas la priorité	Give way
Ralentir	Slow down
Serrez à droite/à gauche	Keep right/left
Sens unique	One way

Petrol (*essence*) and **diesel** (*gas-oil*) are easily obtained. There are plenty of service stations in and around towns, many open 24 hours, but they can be hard to find in the south. Fill up early in the day when travelling in the more remote areas. Most cars take premium grade (*super*); lead-free (*sans-plomb*) is sold only in the larger towns.

Parking. In the centre of most large towns and cities, parking is controlled by *gardiens*, attendants in blue coats, who will guide you into a space, perhaps clean your windscreen and claim a small fee (around 5dh). *Gardiens* are licensed by the local town council, so don't try to avoid paying – they are not hustlers.

Traffic police. Motorcycle police patrol the main highways and sometimes set up checkpoints. Always carry your passport and registration or car-rental documents: you may be asked to show them.

Breakdowns. In most of the towns there should be no problem finding a mechanic to carry out minor repairs. If you happen to break down in the more remote areas, you will have to rely on assistance from passing cars; it can be difficult (and expensive) to find someone to tow you in remote areas.

| My car has broken down. | **Ma voiture est en panne.** |

E

ELECTRICITY

220V/50Hz AC is standard, but older installations of 110V can still be found; check before plugging in. An adaptor for continental-style two-round-pin sockets will be needed, and American 110V appliances will also require a transformer.

EMBASSIES AND CONSULATES *(ambassades/consulats)*

In case of any serious problem (lost passport, stolen money, accident or trouble with the police) contact your consulate or embassy. Citizens of Australia, Ireland and New Zealand should consult the consular facilities of the UK.

Canada: *Embassy* 13 bis, Rue Jaafar Essadik BP709, Agdal, Rabat, tel: 037 68 74 00
UK: *Embassy* 28 Avenue S.A.R. Sidi Mohammed Souissi, Rabat, tel: 037 63 33 33, <www.britain.org.ma>. *Consulates* 36 Rue de la Loire, Polo, Casablanca, tel: 022 85 74 00; Trafalgar House, 9 Rue Amérique du Sud, Tangier, tel: 039 93 69 39

US: *Embassy* 2 Avenue Mohammed el-Fassi, Rabat, tel: 037 76 22 65. *Consulate* 8 Boulevard Moulay Youssef, Casablanca, tel: 022 26 45 50

EMERGENCIES (See also POLICE)

In case of an emergency, telephone:

Police *(police secours)*	19
Ambulance *(samu)*	15/024 44 37 24
Fire brigade *(pompiers)*	15

G

GAY AND LESBIAN TRAVELLERS

Gay travellers are advised to be discreet and cautious. By law, homosexual acts are illegal in Morocco, and punishable by fines and/or imprisonment (6 months to 3 years). That said, Tangier and Marrakesh are still popular destinations among British, American and French gay men, and both have clubs and bars that are openly gay.

GETTING THERE

By Air. From North America: Royal Air Maroc offers direct non-stop service three to five times a week from New York to Casablanca, with connecting flights to Marrakesh, Agadir, Fez and Tangier coordinated to link up with the flight from New York. Royal Air Maroc also flies from Montreal to Casablanca, connecting in New York. No other airline offers a direct service between North America and Morocco. British Airways, KLM, Air France and Iberia operate services between New York and Morocco via Europe; Air France and KLM fly to Morocco from Vancouver, Montreal and Toronto, with stopovers in Europe. Fares are generally lowest on Royal Air Maroc, especially if you fly to destinations in Morocco other than Casablanca. Another option is to fly to London or Paris then pick up a charter flight or low-cost airline to Morocco.

From the UK and Ireland: Royal Air Maroc flies from Heathrow to Casablanca, Tangier, Marrakesh and Agadir; add-on fares are available from other cities in the UK. British Airways (operated by GB Airways) fly from London (Heathrow or Gatwick) to Casablanca, Marrakesh, Agadir, Tangier and now Fez. Charter services and package tours are available from the UK, mainly to Agadir and Marrakesh.

Budget airlines: Royal Air Maroc have their own low-cost airline under the name Atlas Blue, <www.atlas-blue.com>. EasyJet, <www.easyjet.com>, and Ryanair, <www.ryanair.com>, also operate reasonably priced flights from the UK.

By Road. From the UK, the main route from the French ferry ports runs south to Bordeaux and into Spain at Irún, west of the Pyrenees, then on to San Sebastián and Burgos. From there, you take the N-1 to Madrid and the N-IV to Bailán, continuing on the N-IV southwest to Córdoba, then south again to Málaga, and west along the coast to the ferry at Algeciras. Allow for three to four days of steady driving. The driving time can be cut by using the car-ferry service from Plymouth to Santander in northern Spain (a 24-hour trip). From Santander, follow the N-623 to Burgos and then proceed as described above.

By Rail. You will need to travel to Algeciras in Spain *(see opposite)* and catch a ferry from there. Trains to Spain depart from Paris Austerlitz. Allow about two days for the journey from London to Tangier. Morocco is a member of the Inter-Rail Card scheme, which permits either 22 days or 1 month of unlimited rail travel in participating countries (there are three differently priced cards for travellers aged under 26, over 26 and under 12).

By Sea. The main ferry port for Morocco is Algeciras in Spain, a half-hour bus trip from Gibraltar or a two-hour bus journey from

Málaga bus station. There are also far less frequent sea crossings to Morocco from Gibraltar and Málaga themselves (the crossing from Málaga is a lengthy six hours).

From Algeciras, there are ferry crossings throughout the day to Tangier (2 hrs 30 mins) and Ceuta (1 hr 30 mins); Tangier has better connections to public transport in Morocco. If you want to minimise driving time, there are longer, less-frequent car ferry crossings from Sète (France) to Melilla, a Spanish enclave in Morocco.

There are also hydrofoil services, taking a smaller number of vehicles than the ferries, with faster crossing times of 1 hour to Tangier and 30 mins to Ceuta, but they do not run in bad weather (one reason why it can be best to book a single rather than a return ticket). In addition, several hydrofoil and ferry services leave from the quiet, hassle-free port of Tarifa (just west of Algeciras) but they are only available to passengers from the EU.

For information and bookings for ferry or hydrofoil crossings, contact Southern Ferries (30 Churton Street, London SW1V 2LP, tel: 0870 499 1305, freephone UK 0800 082 2010, <www.southern ferries.co.uk>). Tickets for cars should be reserved in advance, especially in high summer when the ports are packed. If you are a foot passenger, there is no need to book in advance.

GUIDES AND TOURS

Official English-speaking guides can be hired through the local tourist office *(see page 126)* and at the better hotels. The guides are usually friendly and knowledgeable and can prove invaluable if your time is limited, especially for navigating the medinas of Fez and Marrakesh.

Official guides carry a brass ID badge, unlike the many unofficial ones (so-called *faux guides*) who hang around the medina gates in tourist towns. It is now illegal for Moroccans to harass tourists, and the amount of hustling has decreased considerably. If you do decide to engage a *faux guide*, even if it's only to get others off your back, be sure to agree in advance exactly what you want to see and the price to be paid. They will invariably try to take you into a shop, where they can earn commission from the owner. If you don't want to buy anything, politely resist entering. On the other hand, if you want a mint tea, a break, or a chance to look at the architecture of one of the many small palaces now turned into carpet showrooms, as well as a chance to learn about Moroccan rugs, by all means, go in. You are not obliged to buy.

H

HEALTH AND MEDICAL CARE (See also EMERGENCIES)

There is no free health care for visitors to Morocco. All medical services must be paid for, and you should not leave home without adequate insurance. The main health hazards are the sun, and contaminated food or water. Protect yourself against the sun, especially in the mountains. Eat only freshly cooked food and drink only bottled water and canned or bottled drinks (without ice). Avoid restaurants with dubious hygiene, undercooked meat, salads, fruit (unless you can peel it yourself), dairy products and tap water.

For minor ailments, seek advice from the local pharmacy. These are usually open during normal shopping hours. Your hotel receptionist should be able to direct you to a late-night pharmacy.

Vaccinations. No compulsory immunisations are required. However, inoculations for tetanus, polio, typhoid and hepatitis-A are recommended for independent travellers intending to travel to rural areas. There is a malaria risk in the province of Taza and the area of Chefchaouen and Larache in summer.

HOLIDAYS (jours fériés)

There are two types of holiday in Morocco: secular and religious. Banks, post offices, government offices, and many other businesses will be closed on the following secular holidays:

1 January	New Year's Day
11 January	Independence Manifesto Day
1 May	Labour Day
23 May	National Holiday *(Fête Nationale)*
30 July	Feast of the Throne
14 August	Reunification Day
21 August	The King's Birthday and Youth Day
6 November	Anniversary of the Green March
18 November	Independence Day

Religious holidays are marked by two (or three) days off and vary annually. Check with the tourist office *(see page 126)* for details.

The Muslim new year is the **Fatih Mouharam**. Ten days later, the **Achoura** commemorates the assassination of Hussein, grandson of Mohammed. **Aid el Mouloud** celebrates the anniversary of the birth of the Prophet Mohammed. After four weeks of fasting for Ramadan, the **Aid el Fitr** or **Aid es Seghir** (small feast) is marked by three days of holiday. Seventy days later, for the **Aid el Adha**, or **Aid el Kebir** (great feast), which commemorates the sacrifice of Abraham, each family kills a sheep and gives part of it to the poor.

L

LANGUAGE

The official language of Morocco is Arabic, but a large proportion of the population, especially in the cities, also speaks fluent French; most signs and street names are in both languages. If you can get by in French you should have no communication problems, except in remote Berber villages, where the Berber language is still spoken. Although written Arabic is the same across the Arab world, the spoken dialect of Moroccan Arabic is quite distinctive, and travellers who have learned the Arabic of the Middle East may struggle to communicate.

Although Moroccans will not expect you to know any Arabic and will probably greet you in French or English (see phrases throughout this section for help with French), it is polite to learn at least a few basic phrases of Arabic.

hello (informal)	*bonjour*	**labes**
hello (formal)	*bonjour*	**as salaam alaykum**
goodbye	*au revoir*	**bslemah**
yes/no	*oui, non*	**na'am, la**
perhaps	*peut-être*	**yimkin**
please	*s'il vous plaît*	**min fadlak**
thank you	*merci*	**shokran**

MEDIA

Newspapers and magazines *(journaux/revues)*. Locally produced French-language publications include *Le Matin du Sahara*, *L'Opinion* and *Maroc Soir*, all of which provide a thin diet of North African and international news and sport. The French dailies, *Le Monde* and *Le Figaro*, and the *International Herald Tribune* are also widely available on city newsstands. British newspapers can be found a day or two after publication in the larger cities and resorts.

Radio and television *(radio/télévision)*. With a short-wave radio you will be able to pick up the English-language broadcasts of the BBC World Service and Voice of America. Otherwise, local stations offer a choice of traditional Moroccan music, or news, sports and current affairs in Arabic or French. In the north, it is easy to pick up stations from Gibraltar, Spain, Portugal and Italy.

The better hotels (three stars plus) have TVs in the rooms, some with satellite channels. The two Moroccan TV channels broadcast in Arabic, with the evening news repeated in French and Spanish.

MONEY

Currency *(monnaie)*. The unit of currency is the dirham (dh), which is divided into 100 centimes. Centimes are occasionally referred to as francs. Notes come in denominations of 20dh, 50dh, 100dh and 200dh, and coins in 5, 10, 20 and 50 centimes, 1dh, 5dh and 10dh.

The dirham is a soft currency, and the exchange rate is controlled by the government, so it is the same everywhere.

Banks and currency exchange *(banques, change)*. Approximate banking hours are Mon–Fri 8 or 8.30am–11.30pm or noon and 2 or 3pm–5 or 6pm; some open 8am–2 or 3pm in summer. Changing money takes time, as you may have to queue twice, first to do the paperwork, then again to collect the cash. In some of the most popular tourist resorts, such as Tangier, Marrakesh and Agadir, there are independent exchange booths *(bureaux de change)*, which provide a faster service. They are open daily 8am–8pm.

Travellers' cheques *(chèques de voyage)*. These are accepted at the banks listed above, though smaller branches may refuse to cash them. You will need your passport and sometimes the purchase receipts, too; a small commission is charged on each cheque.

Credit cards *(cartes de crédit)*. Major credit cards are accepted in the better hotels (three-star and above) and restaurants in the larger cities, by tourist shops, car-rental firms and larger petrol stations.

ATM machines. These are plentiful in all main towns. BMCE banks have ATMs at Place Mohammed V in Fez and Place des Nations Unies in Casablanca, and on Rue Bab Agnaou, near Jemaa el Fna in Marrakesh. The exchange rate is better than for cash or travellers' cheques, but check charges with your bank before leaving.

I want to change some pounds/dollars	**Je voudrais changer des livres sterling/dollars**
Do you accept travellers' cheques/this credit card?	**Acceptez-vous les chèques de voyage/cette carte de crédit?**

O

OPENING HOURS (*heures d'ouverture*)

Banks: variable but generally Mon–Fri 8am–noon and 2–4pm; 8 or 9am–2 or 3pm during Ramadan and July–August.
Museums: generally 9am–noon and 3–6pm; most close on Tues.
Shops: Mon–Sat 8.30 or 9am–noon and 2.30–6.30 or 7pm. Some close Fri, notably in the medinas; others close Sat.

Are you open tomorrow? **Est-ce que vous ouvrez demain?**

P

POLICE (See also EMERGENCIES)

Morocco's civil police, the Sûreté Nationale, wear blue uniforms and patrol urban areas. *Gendarmes* are responsible for rural areas and wear grey uniforms. There is a police station in most towns. If you want to report a crime, it is a good idea to get a fluent French or Arabic speaker to help you – ask at your hotel or the local tourist office. Highway checkpoints are patrolled by Gendarmes (see also DRIVING). In the event of an emergency, dial **19** for the police.

Where's the nearest   **Où se trouve le commissariat**
police station?   **de police le plus proche?**

POST OFFICES (*bureaux de poste*)

Post Offices, marked by a yellow sign with the letters PTT, handle mail, parcels, telegrams and telephone calls. Hours are generally 8.30am–6.30pm Mon–Sat, but smaller branches close for lunch, from noon–2.30 or 3pm and at noon on Sat. Post offices in larger cities have counters that stay open 24 hours a day. Postage stamps *(timbres)* are also on sale at tobacconists' kiosks *(tabacs)* and hotel desks, and at tourist shops that sell postcards.

PUBLIC TRANSPORT

Buses. There are a variety of bus companies. CTM buses, <www.ctm.co.ma>, are fast and reliable with numbered seats. Supratours Express buses are the best that run on major routes. Operated by the train company ONCF, they are very comfortable, fast and reliable. There are several other larger private bus companies, including SATAS and Trans Ghazala.

Except on the express services, which have air-conditioning and videos, bus travel over long distances can be uncomfortable. If you have a choice, it is better to take the train. Tourist offices and the main bus stations will have information on routes and timetables.

Grands taxis. A faster and slightly more comfortable alternative to the bus for shorter journeys between towns is the *grand taxi*. This is usually a large Mercedes Benz that shuttles back and forth along a set route; in most cases with six passengers. There are no fixed departure times; the taxi departs when all the seats are full. To find a place, you simply turn up at the 'terminal' (the tourist office or your hotel will tell you where this is; it is often next to the main bus station) and ask the drivers. Fares are per person for a full car; if you fear being overcharged ask other passengers (or your hotel receptionist) what the standard fare is. Fares are only slightly higher than on the bus. If you pay double you can have the front seat to yourself.

Petits taxis. These are small cars (often a Fiat Uno or a Peugeot 205) that operate as city taxis for short trips within town for a maximum of three passengers. Hail one in the street or pick one up at a taxi rank; in the larger cities you can order one by telephone. The drivers sometimes forget to switch on the meters for foreigners, so you may want to negotiate the fare before getting in. Fares are increased by 50 percent after dark but are still very cheap by European standards.

Trains. The national rail company, the ONCF (Office National des Chemins de Fer, <www.oncf.ma>), maintains a limited but efficient rail network. It extends from Tangier south to Marrakesh and east to Oujda at the Algerian border, linking Fez, Meknes, Rabat and Casablanca. Mainline trains are modern, comfortable and inexpensive. Where possible, choose a *rapide* service, as these are faster and more comfortable than *ordinaire* trains. To be assured of a seat, you'll have to upgrade to first class.

R

RELIGION

Morocco is a Muslim country but is very tolerant of other religions. Christians account for about 1 percent of the population; there are Roman Catholic churches in most large towns and Anglican churches in Tangier, Rabat and Casablanca. Jewish synagogues can also be found in the main cities. Details of local religious services can be obtained from the local tourist office (see TOURIST INFORMATION). Islam teaches social conservatism, and, away from the beach, men and women should always dress modestly and avoid shorts; women should avoid wearing miniskirts and revealing tops (see WOMEN TRAVELLERS).

The king is the country's spiritual leader, so never make jokes about the monarch. Non-Muslims are forbidden to enter mosques, *koubbas* (shrines) and most other Islamic monuments, except the courtyard of Moulay Ismail's tomb in Meknes, the Bou Inania Medersa in Fez, the Mausoleum of Mohammed V and Hassan II in Rabat, and the Hassan II and Tin Mal mosques. If you plan to visit any of these you should dress conservatively. Do not photograph anyone without asking permission and do not attempt to photograph Muslims at prayer.

T

TELEPHONES *(téléphones)*

Domestic and international telephone calls can be made from phone boxes *(cabines)* on the street or in a main post ofice. They take 1dh and 5dh coins or phone cards, available from post offices and some grocery stores. Private pay-phone booths *(téléboutiques)* are widespread; clean and efficient, they cost little more than a pay phone on the street.

To make a call within Morocco, lift the receiver, insert your coins, and dial the number, including the area code, even if the call is local (area codes are included in all telephone numbers listed in this guide). The ringing tone is a long single tone.

To make an international call, dial 00 and wait for a second tone, then dial the country code (44 for the UK, 1 for the US and Canada) and the full number, omitting the initial zero from the area code. To make a reverse-charge (collect) call, dial 12 for an international operator. The code for Morocco is 212.

TIME ZONES

Morocco operates on Greenwich Mean Time all the year round. The following table shows the time differences in various international cities in summer.

New York	London	Morocco	Sydney	Los Angeles
7am	1pm	**noon**	10pm	4am

TIPPING

It is customary to offer a tip *(pourboire)* for services rendered. A few dirhams is the norm for café waiters, porters, parking or gas station attendants and the attendants *(gardiens)* at monuments and museums; while restaurant waiters often get 10–20dh on top of any service charge. Porters at airports and ferry terminals usually charge per piece of luggage. Taxi drivers do not generally expect a tip.

TOURIST INFORMATION *(office de tourisme, syndicat d'initiative)*

The Moroccan National Tourist Office (Office National Marocain de Tourisme, or ONMT) has branches throughout the country. Staff can help with accommodation and provide official guides and interpreters, but standards of service vary. Most towns have a Syndicat d'Initiative, an information office run by the local authorities.

Offices open 8.30am–4.30pm, and close Sat afternoon and Sun.

Rabat: (head office) corner of Rue Oued el-Makhazine and Rue Zellaka, 3km (2 miles) southwest of the centre, tel: 037 67 39 18

Agadir: Unit A, Place Prince Héritier Sidi Mohammed (the main shopping centre), tel: 028 84 63 77; and Boulevard Mohammed V, tel: 028 82 18 21

Casablanca: 55 Rue Omar Slaoui, tel: 022 27 11 77; and 98 Boulevard Mohammed V, tel: 022 22 15 24

Fez: Place de la Résistance, tel: 035 62 34 60; and Place Mohammed V, tel: 035 65 43 70

Marrakesh: Place Abdelmoumen Ben Ali, tel: 024 43 62 39

Meknes: 27 Place Administrative, tel: 035 51 60 22

Tangier: 29 Boulevard Pasteur, tel: 039 94 80 50

The ONMT also has several overseas offices:

Australia: 2/11 West St, North Sydney NSW 2060, tel: 02 9922 4999

Canada: 2001 Rue Université 1460, Montreal, Quebec QH3A 2A6, tel: (514) 842 8111

UK: 205 Regent Street, London W1R 7DE, tel: 020 7437 0073, email: <mnto@btconnect.com>
US: Suite 1201, 20 East 46th Street, New York NY 10017, tel: (212) 557 2520
PO Box 2263, Lake Buena Vista, Orlando, FL 32830, tel: (407) 827 5335

WATER

Although tap water is considered to be safe in most parts of Morocco, it is advisable to avoid drinking it – and to avoid ice cubes in your drinks. Bottled mineral water is widely available – Sidi Harazem and Sidi Ali are the most popular brands of still mineral water; Oulmes is carbonated.

WEBSITES

www.tourisme-marocain.com National Tourist Office (in French).
www.morocco.com Includes hotel booking and travel tips.
www.moroccotoday.net Moroccan English-language newspaper.

WOMEN TRAVELLERS

Foreign women travelling in Morocco are often subject to harassment from local men. A woman accompanied by a man is less likely to attract unwanted attention but is not immune from it. That said, the majority of Moroccans are courteous and show genuine hospitality.

The way you dress is crucial; do not wear shorts and a skimpy top except in beach resorts. Dress modestly in trousers or a skirt that sits below the knee, with loose-fitting tops with sleeves. Avoid eye contact with local men, and ignore any rude comments. Wear a headscarf when you visit a mosque.

Recommended Hotels

If you're visiting Morocco on a package tour, all your accommodation will most likely be arranged for you in advance. Our selection of hotels is therefore biased towards the independent traveller, concentrating on towns and cities that make useful base-camps or stopovers during a tour of the country. *(See also page 106.)*

As a basic guide we have used the symbols below to indicate prices for a double room with bath (breakfast in many hotels is extra). Major credit cards are accepted unless otherwise stated.

€€€€€	1,500 dirhams and above
€€€€	750–1500 dirhams
€€€	400–750 dirhams
€€	250–400 dirhams
€	less than 250 dirhams

AGADIR

Hotel Kamal €€€ *Avenue Hassan II, tel: 028 84 28 17, <www.hotelkamal.ma>.* Spotless and well-equipped modern hotel with friendly staff, close to the city centre. The hotel has a pool, and rooms have TV and bath. 128 rooms.

Sindibad €€ *Place Lahcen Tamri, tel: 028 82 34 77, fax: 028 84 24 74.* A well-run hotel in a lively quarter. Restaurant, rooftop pool. 55 rooms with bath, phone and TV.

Sofitel Agadir €€€€€ *Baie des Palmiers, Ben Sergao, tel: 028 82 00 88, <www.sofitel.com>.* A huge luxury resort right on the seafront, offering all the amenities you'd expect of a five-star hotel. Excellent food. 273 rooms.

ASILAH

Patio de la Luna €€€ *12 Rue Zellaka, tel: 039 41 60 74.* A delightful *maison d'hôtes* (guesthouse) in a great location just outside the city wall. Rooms are generally small but tastefully furnished and have en-suite bathrooms. 8 rooms.

CASABLANCA

Hyatt Regency €€€€€ *Place des Nations Unies, tel: 022 43 12 34, <www.casablanca.hyatt.com>*. In a busy location in the heart of the commercial district, this dramatically designed contemporary 5-star edifice has a pool, squash court, health club and a choice of restaurants. 255 rooms.

Ibis Moussafir €€ *Place de la Gare, tel: 022 40 19 84, <www.ibishotel.com>*. Modern, efficient hotel with pool. If you come to Casablanca by train in order to catch a next-day flight, this is a convenient place to stay overnight; take the train from Central Station next door directly to the airport. Book ahead. 118 rooms.

Kenzi Basma €€€€ *35 Avenue Moulay Hassan I, tel: 022 22 33 23, <www.hotel-kenzi-basma.com>*. About a block from Place des Nations Unies, with good-value, balconied rooms; those on the seventh and eighth floors have fine views. 115 rooms.

Royal Mansour Meridien €€€€€ *27 Avenue des Far, tel: 022 31 30 11, <www.starwoodhotels.com>*. Centred on a glass-enclosed winter garden complete with cascades, this is the most exotic of the 5-star hotels in town. Moroccan decor, beautiful rooms, a good Moroccan restaurant, plus health club, solarium and sauna. 182 rooms.

Sheraton Casablanca €€€€€ *100 Avenue des Far, tel: 022 43 94 94, <www.sheraton.com/casablanca>*. Expect beautiful contemporary decor, marble baths, a third-floor terrace pool and efficient staff in this 5-star hotel. Special rooms for disabled guests and non-smokers. 286 rooms.

Transatlantique €€ *79 Rue Chaouia, tel: 022 29 45 51, <www.transatcasa.com>*. Charming, centrally located hotel, in a magnificent art-deco building, with spacious and comfortable rooms. Two restaurants, bar and nightclub with belly dancers. 52 rooms.

CHAOUEN (CHEFCHAOUEN)

Dar Terrae €€€ *M'Daka, Quartier Andalous, tel: 039 98 75 98,* *<www.darterrae.com>.* Andalucian-style house converted into a stylish *riad* hotel, with beautiful roof terraces overlooking the town. 6 rooms.

Hostal Gernika € *49 Rue Onssar, tel: 039 98 74 34.* Run by an energetic Basque woman proprietor, this tiny hotel in the upper town is pleasant, attractively decorated and spotlessly clean. 9 rooms, 3 with private bathrooms. Cash only.

Parador €€€ *Place de Makhzen, tel: 039 98 61 36, <www.* *fres.hotel-parador.com>.* Offers comfortable modern rooms, a smoky bar where a few older local men hang out, and a pool (summer only). Good location beside the medina's main square. 55 rooms.

ESSAOUIRA

Casa Lila € *94 Rue Mohamed el Qorry, Bab Marrakech, tel: 024 47 55 45, <www.splendia.com/riad-casa-lila>.* Beautifully renovated *riad* hotel with pastel-toned rooms and large bathrooms. The courtyard and terraces are filled with palms and banana trees. 10 rooms.

Dar L'Oussia €€€€ *4 Rue Mohammed Ben Messaoud, tel: 024 78 37 56, <www.dar-loussia.net>.* Large, spacious *riad* down a backstreet at the bay entrance to the medina. Simply furnished, pleasantly decorated rooms are arranged on three levels around a central courtyard. The *riad* has a bar and a good restaurant on the ground floor. 24 rooms.

L'Heure Bleue €€€€€ *2 Rue Ibn Batuta, tel: 024 78 34 34, <www.* *heure-bleue.com>.* This African colonial gem tops the list of hotels in Essaouira. Its high price tag is wholly justified by impeccable yet unfussy service, excellent Moroccan cuisine, sumptuous bedrooms and bathrooms, and superb views over the medina. 35 rooms.

Madada Mogador €€€€–€€€€€ *5 Rue Youssef El Fassi, tel: 024 47 55 12, <www.madada.com>.* Chic boutique hotel close to the town square and overlooking the bay. The hotel's guest rooms are decorated in a cool contemporary style and some have private terraces. One of the most fashionable addresses in Essaouira. 7 rooms.

Villa Maroc €€€–€€€€ *10 Rue Abdellah Ben Yassine, tel: 024 47 61 47, <www.villa-maroc.com>.* Superb, atmospheric hotel in a converted double mansion, with variety of designer rooms and suites arranged around two courtyards. Excellent staff; in-house dining offering well-prepared Moroccan specialities and a wonderful roof terrace with panoramic views. 22 rooms and suites, each unique.

FEZ

Amor € *31 Rue Arabie Saoudite, tel: 035 62 27 24.* In a central but fairly quiet Ville Nouvelle location, this hotel has neat, clean rooms with private bathrooms. Restaurant and bar. 35 rooms. Cash only.

Grand Hotel €€€ *Boulevard Chefchaouni, tel: 035 93 20 26, email: <grandhotel@fesnet.ma>.* This was once the great 1930s art-deco hotel of Fez. Very central, with comfortable air-conditioned rooms and baths, a short block from the restaurants and cafés of Boulevard Mohammed V. Underground parking. 84 rooms.

Hotel Batha €€€ *Place Batha, tel: 035 63 64 37.* Functional hotel noted for its excellent location at the gateway to Fez-el-Bali. The hotel has adequate, but unexceptional, air-conditioned rooms and a courtyard pool. 60 rooms.

Ibis Moussafir €€€ *Place de la Gare, tel: 035 65 19 02, <www.ibis hotel.com>.* Modern, efficient hotel with pool in the Ibis chain. Convenient location close to the railway station. 125 rooms.

Jnan Palace €€€€–€€€€€ *Avenue Ahmed Chaouki, tel: 035 65 22 30 <www.sogatour.ma>.* Large and rather opulent modern hotel set in extensive grounds. One of the best of the business-style hotels in Fez, with a wide range of amenities. 244 rooms.

La Maison Bleue €€€€€ *2 Place de l'Istiqlal, tel: 035 63 60 52, <www.maisonbleue.com>*. Antique-filled suites and rooms in the former mansion of one of Fez's leading families. Superb location, accessible by taxi, a 4-minute walk to the gates of Fez el Bali. 6 rooms.

Nouzha €€€ *7 Rue Hassan Dkhissi, tel: 035 64 00 02, fax: 035 64 00 84.* Built in 1996, and located at Place d'Atlas, 10 minutes' walk from the heart of the Ville Nouvelle, this hotel has an impressive Moorish lobby and spacious air-conditioned guest rooms. 59 rooms.

Riad Arabesque €€€ *30 Derb al-Mitter, near the Palais Jamaï, tel: 035 63 53 21, <www.arabesquehotel.com>*. Sumptuous *riad* hotel, with spacious rooms around a central courtyard, which has an atmospheric Moroccan restaurant at night. 7 rooms.

Riad Louna €€€€ *21 Derb Serraj, Talaa Sghira, Bab Boujloud, Medina, tel: 035 74 19 85, <www.riadlouna.com>*. Gorgeous Belgian-owned *riad* hotel. Comfortable rooms are set around a magnificent courtyard filled with orange and apricot trees. The owners love the city, will cook dinner if you wish, and even organise cookery classes. 8 rooms.

Sofitel Palais Jamai €€€€€ *Bâb el Guissa, Medina, tel: 035 63 43 31, <www.sofitel.com>*. One of Fez's top hotels, incorporating a 19th-century Vizier's palace, with panoramic views overlooking the medina. Facilities include a pool, gardens, the luxurious Moroccan-style restaurant Al Fassia, and a good French restaurant. The medina location can be confining at night. 133 rooms.

Splendid €€ *9 Rue Abdelkrim el Khattabi, tel: 035 62 21 48, fax: 035 65 48 92.* Centrally located, competent, busy hotel with air conditioning, modest guest rooms and a small pool. 70 rooms. Some credit cards.

Volubilis €€€ *Avenue Allal Ben Abdellah, tel: 035 62 30 98, fax: 035 62 11 25.* Set around a lush garden with swimming pool, this hotel offers comfortable rooms, tennis and basketball courts, and a fitness centre. Heavily booked by groups; reserve well in advance. 130 rooms. Some credit cards.

MARRAKESH

Dar Al Sultan €€€€ *26 Derb el-Arsa, Riad Zitoun Jdid, Medina, tel: 071 08 36 08, <www.daralsultan.com>*. Gorgeous *riad* with well-preserved traditional architecture, *zellige* tiling and carved wood. The spaces have a very contemporary feel, but are cosy and tranquil. Delightful owner and central location. 3 rooms.

Gallia €€€ *30 Rue de la Recette, Medina, tel: 024 44 59 13, fax: 024 44 48 53*. Simple, bright rooms, some with shared baths, arranged around two delightful courtyards at the edge of the medina. Well-run and popular; book two months ahead. 19 rooms.

Jnane Tamsna €€€€€ *Douar Abiad, Palmeraie, tel: 024 32 94 23, <www.jnanetamsna.com>*. Set in a lush organic garden, the four villas are decorated by one of Marrakesh's top designers, with sumptuous rooms, large bathrooms and a pool each. Drinks and meals are served in different places in this oasis according to the mood and weather. The food, mostly homegrown, is excellent. 20 rooms.

Palmeraie Golf Palace €€€€€ *Circuit de la Palmeraie, tel: 024 36 87 22, fax: 024 30 50 50, <www.pgp.co.ma>*. A golfer's paradise: five-star luxury with rooms and suites overlooking the gardens, Robert Trent Jones golf course or Atlas Mountains. 314 rooms.

Riad Farnatchi €€€€€ *2 Derb el-Farnatchi, Qa'at Benahid, Medina, tel: 024 38 49 10, <www.riadfarnatchi.com>*. Three small *riads* converted into a superb small luxury hotel, with magnificent suites and a free *hammam* for residents. The exceptional manager can organise almost anything you fancy. 5 rooms.

Riad Nejma Lounge €€€€ *45 Derb Sidi M'hamed el-Haj, Bab Doukkala, Medina, tel: 024 38 23 41, <www.riad-nejmalounge. com>*. Fashionable *riad* popular with a younger crowd. The stylish ultra-white background is offset by bright colours in the furnishings and lots of palms and exotic plants. Laid-back atmosphere and a great roof terrace for lounging. 6 rooms.

Riyad Edward €€€€€ *10 Derb Marestane, Zaouia Abbassia, Bab Taghzoute, Medina, tel: 024 38 97 97/061 25 23 28, <www.riyad edward.com>*. Unusually large *riad* with a spacious, tiled courtyard, a pool and a 100-year-old cypress tree. Loads of terraces, reading corners and little salons to relax in. The old *hammam* takes a few hours to heat up, so warn the housekeeper in advance. 10 rooms.

Sherazade €€–€€€ *3 Derb Jemaa, Riad Zitoun Kedim, tel/fax: 024 42 93 05, <www.hotelsherazade.com>*. Off a main medina street just south of Jemaa el Fna, this reasonably priced delightful courtyard *riad* is spotlessly clean and run by a helpful multi-lingual staff. 22 rooms, some with shared bathroom.

Tchaïkana €€€€ *25 Derb el-Ferrane, Azbest, Medina, tel: 024 38 51 50, <www.tchaikana.com>*. Beautiful, tastefully decorated *riad* run by a Belgian couple. The large elegant rooms overlook an atmospheric courtyard, which looks even better at night. 5 rooms.

Tlaata wa Sitteen €–€€ *63 Derb el-Ferrane, Riad Laarous, Medina, tel: 024 38 30 26, <www.tlaatawasitteen.com>*. Great budget option run by charming Moroccans who warmly welcome families into their traditional *riad*. Rooms are simple but stylish, with shared *tadelakht* bathrooms. Dinner available on request. 6 rooms.

MEKNES

Majestic €–€€ *19 Avenue Mohammed V, tel: 035 52 20 35, email: <majestic.hotel@excite.fr>*. A no-frills but tidy hotel in the heart of the Ville Nouvelle with spacious airy rooms and a touch of character. Some rooms have en-suite facilities; avoid the noisy rooms at the back of the hotel. 40 rooms.

Transatlantique €€€€ *Rue el Meiniyine, tel: 035 52 50 50, fax: 035 52 00 57*. The best hotel in town, set high on a hill in a residential part of the Ville Nouvelle, with a view of the medina across the valley. Two restaurants, two swimming pools and a rather faded grandeur. 121 rooms.

OUARZAZATE

Dar Kamar €€€€ *45 Kasbah Taourirt, tel: 024 88 87 33, <www. darkamar.com>*. This wonderful *riad* has been restored using traditional materials and is filled with the Spanish owner's collection of *objets d'art*. Great views from the rooftop terrace and excellent food. Camping trips organised. 12 rooms.

Dar Daif €€€€ *Douar Talmasla, tel: 024 85 42 32, <www.dardaif. com>*. Rustic kasbah-style hotel on the edge of town, overlooking the palmery and the stork's kasbah. Well-run and beautifully decorated using local crafts. 11 rooms.

RABAT

Balima €€ *Boulevard Mohammed V, tel: 037 70 86 25, fax: 037 70 74 50*. Old-fashioned hotel, with faded grandeur, conveniently situated by the Moroccan Parliament. Rooms are spacious and comfortable, with high ceilings. Popular terrace café. 71 rooms.

La Tour Hassan €€€€€ *26 Rue Chellah BP14, tel: 037 23 90 00, <www.latourhassan.com>*. In the heart of the city, this hotel has stunning Moroccan decor – mosaics, marble, mirrors and arcades – a magnificent garden, two excellent restaurants and a pool. 139 rooms.

Majestic €€ *121 Avenue Hassan II, tel: 037 72 29 97, email: <majestic@welcome.net.ma>*. Well-located, friendly hotel with spotless rooms with private facilities. Perhaps the best of the budget options in Rabat. 40 rooms.

TANGIER

El Minzah €€€€€ *85 Rue de la Liberté, tel: 039 93 58 85, <www. elminzah.com>*. Five-star establishment, set amid lush gardens with fine views over the bay. Two restaurants (one Moroccan), atmospheric bar, pool, fitness centre. 140 rooms.

El Muniria € *1 Rue Magellan, tel: 039 93 53 37.* Good cheap option with a bit of faded style. This was once a popular hangout of Beatnik poets and writers. Below the hotel lies the sporadically popular Tanger Inn, which is even more faded. 6 rooms.

La Tangerina €€€–€€€€ *19 Riad Sultan (Kasbah), tel :039 94 77 31, <www.latangerina.com>.* Wonderful *riad* perched high above the Kasbah, offering panoramic views of the city and the Straits of Gibraltar. Very friendly and lovingly restored. 8 rooms.

TAROUDANNT

Palais Salam €€€€ *Kasbah of Taroudannt, tel: 028 85 25 01, <www.palaissalamtaroudant.com>.* Former pasha's palace set amid luxuriant gardens, with a pool, two fine restaurants, a bar and tennis courts. The rooms in the garden pavilions and towers are worth the extra cost. 140 rooms.

Résidence Riad Maryam €€ *Derb Maalen Mohammed, off Avenue Mohammed V, tel: 066 12 72 85, <www.riadmaryam.fr.fm>.* Popular family-run guesthouse with clean comfortable rooms around a shady courtyard full of trees and birds. The Moroccan owner is always ready to help you discover his city. 8 rooms.

Riad Hida €€€ *Oued Berhil, 40km (25 miles) east of Taroudannt, tel: 028 53 10 44, <www.riadhida.com>.* This 19th-century pasha's palace is now an atmospheric hotel, with large rooms overlooking a lush garden with peacocks and a fine pool. Good value. 12 rooms.

ZAGORA

Riad Lamane €€€ *Amezrou, tel: 024 84 83 88, <www.riadlamane. com>.* Very comfortable and large rooms furnished in local style with air-conditioning and heating. Three restaurants, terraces, garden and swimming pool. 20 rooms.

Recommended Restaurants

A classic Moroccan meal, served at low tables, is eaten with fingers and thumb of the right hand, but hotels and restaurants will not insist. The following is just an introduction to the many restaurants in Morocco. Note that booking ahead is recommended, particularly in Casablanca and Marrakesh. To give an idea of the price of a three-course meal for two, including service but excluding drinks, we have used the following:

€€€€	600 dirhams and above
€€€	300–600 dirhams
€€	100–300 dirhams
€	less than 100 dirhams

The food markets of the medinas are good places to try Moroccan fare – from wonderful breads, cheeses, olives and stuffed dried fruits and pastries to freshly cooked fish and kebabs, all at very low prices.

AGADIR

La Scala €€€ *Rue du Oued Souss, tel: 028 84 67 73.* Open daily for lunch and dinner. Excellent upmarket Moroccan restaurant with a cosmopolitan atmosphere and delicious food. Book ahead.

Mimi La Brochette €€ *Rue de la Plage, tel: 028 84 03 87.* Open daily for lunch and dinner. At the north end of the beach, Mimi's cooking is a real treat, with Jewish, French and Spanish influences. Large menu includes the best *brochettes* (meat skewers) in town.

Restaurant du Port €€–€€€ *Agadir Port, tel: 028 84 37 08.* Open daily for lunch and dinner. Licensed restaurant doing excellent fresh fish and seafood. Bring your passport to enter the harbour zone. Major credit cards.

Yacout *Avenue du 29 Février, tel: 028 84 65 88.* Fine patisserie-bakery that is justly renowned for its wonderful *cornes de gazelle* (pastry crescents stuffed with ground nuts and cinnamon).

ASILAH

Casa Garcia €€–€€€ *Rue Moulay Hassan Ben El Mehdi, tel: 039 41 74 65.* Open daily for lunch and dinner. Licensed restaurant serving excellent fish dishes just around the corner from Plaza Zalaka. Considered to be the best restaurant in Asilah.

CASABLANCA

A Ma Bretagne €€€€ *Boulevard de la Corniche, Sidi Abderrahman, tel: 022 94 41 55.* Open Mon–Sat for lunch and dinner. Closed in August. Overlooking the sea, 10km (6 miles) west of the city centre, this is one of Morocco's (and indeed Africa's) best French restaurants, run by Maître Cuisinier de France, André Halbert. Inventive menu strong on fish and seafood. Terrace dining in good weather. Major credit cards.

Al Mounia €€–€€€ *95 Rue de Prince Moulay Abdallah, tel: 022 22 26 69.* Open Mon–Sat for lunch and dinner. The city's premier restaurant for Moroccan food, with superb *pastilla* and *tajines*. Decor is exotic. Pleasant garden dining area. Major credit cards.

Ostrea €€–€€€ *Port de Pêche, tel: 022 44 13 90.* Open daily for lunch and dinner. At this informal place you choose your fish before it is cooked. The *tajines*, paella and fish soup are justly renowned. Reservation is essential. Major credit cards.

Le Quai du Jazz €€€ *25 Rue Ahmed El Mokri, tel : 022 94 25 37.* Open Mon–Fri for lunch and dinner; Sat dinner only; closed Sun. Stylish brasserie serving French cuisine in the heart of the city centre. Excellent food, service, a comprehensive wine list and live jazz on selected nights.

CHAOUEN (CHEFCHAOUEN)

Tissemlal €€ *Zenkat et-Tergui, Medina, tel: 039 98 61 53.* Open daily for lunch and dinner. Great French-Moroccan restaurant in a beautiful house in the medina. They also have a few rooms upstairs.

ESSAOUIRA

Chalet de la Plage €€–€€€ *Boulevard Mohammed V, tel: 024 47 59 72.* Reliable fish restaurant overlooking the town's beach. Try to get a table on the terrace where the sea virtually laps at your feet. Licensed. Major credit cards.

Elizir €€€ *1 Rue d'Agadir, tel: 024 47 21 03.* Convivial Italian/Moroccan restaurant in a typical Essaouiran townhouse in the medina. Decorated with art-deco artifacts and adorned with an eclectic mix of 1970s objets d'art, this friendly restaurant serves a menu of simple pasta dishes and authentic *tajines*.

Chez Sam €–€€ *Port de Pêche, tel: 024 47 65 13.* Open daily for lunch and dinner. This Essaouira institution specialises in fresh fish and seafood, served in cosy surroundings. You can watch the fishing boats from your table. Bar and wine list. Major credit cards.

Ristorante Silvestro €€€ *70 Rue Laalouj, tel: 024 47 35 55.* Open daily for lunch and dinner. Good-value Italian restaurant noted for its open kitchen and excellent ingredients imported from Italy. The restaurant is owned and run by chef Silvestro who traded his hectic Milanese restaurant for a quieter life in Essaouira.

FEZ

Al Fassia €€€€ *Hotel Palais Jamaï, Bab Guissa, Medina, tel: 035 63 43 31.* Dinner only. Perhaps the best and most refined restaurant in town, serving all the typical Fassi specialities – all of which need to be ordered 24 hours in advance. Great food, good folkloric show and a wonderful terrace overlooking the whole medina.

Dar Saada €€–€€€€ *21 Souk Attarine, tel: 035 63 73 70.* Open daily for lunch only. The most affordable of the palace restaurants, this place is in a great location, in the heart of the medina's markets, near the Kairouyine Mosque. Good food, with a wide range of fixed-price meals (including fish) and lavish decor. Popular with tour groups. Major credit cards.

Fish Friture € *138 Boulevard Mohammed V, tel: 035 94 06 99.* Open daily 11am–3pm and 6pm–midnight. Congenial restaurant, serving fresh fish and Moroccan dishes. Owner, Monsieur Lazarak, is a skilled guide who offers excellent advice and information. Good *pastilla* and spaghetti with seafood. Major credit cards.

La Kasbah € *Near the Bab Boujeloud, Fes el-Bali.* Open daily 9am–11pm. Budget Moroccan restaurant that serves good *tajines*, couscous and grilled meats in a salon with low tables or, even better, on two atmospheric terraces that have great views over the crowds in the medina. No alcohol but the mint tea is excellent.

La Maison Bleue €€€€ *2 Place de l'Istiqlal, tel: 035 63 60 52.* Dinner only by arrangement. This intimate, aristocratic mansion *(see page 132)* has one of the best restaurants in town offering a refined Moroccan menu. Wine list and soft Gnaoua and Andalusian music. Major credit cards.

Zagora €€–€€€ *5 Boulevard Mohammed V, tel: 035 94 06 86.* Open daily for lunch and dinner. Quality Moroccan and Continental cuisine served in a tranquil, dignified atmosphere. Ask about off-menu regional Moroccan specialities such as Essaouira chicken. Large portions and heavenly *pastilla*. Major credit cards.

MARRAKESH

Al-Fassia €€€ *55 Boulevard Zerktouni, Ville Nouvelle, tel: 024 43 40 60.* Hugely popular Moroccan restaurant preparing such delights as chicken-and-caramalised-pumpkin *tajine* and gorgeous Moroccan salads. Booking essential. Licensed. Major credit cards.

Argana Café Restaurant € *1 Place Jemaa el Fna, tel: 024 44 53 50.* Open daily 10am–midnight. Wonderful *tajines*, couscous dishes and salads served on terraces overlooking Jemaa el Fna. Very affordable prices. Cash only.

Café des Épices € *Place Rahba Qedima, tel: 024 39 17 70.* Open daily 8am–10pm. The best place in the medina to watch the world go by. Great mint tea and a limited but delicious lunch menu. Laid-back atmosphere and really good music. Wifi connection. Cash only.

Casa Lalla €€€€ *16 Derb Jamaa, off Riad Zitoun el-Qedim, Medina, tel: 024 42 97 57, <www.casalalla.com>.* Originally the creation of Michelin-starred British chef Richard Neat, this guesthouse-cum-gastronomic restaurant, which is now under French ownership, is noted for its daily *menu dégustation* of multiple courses served at 8pm sharp. Booking essential. Prepare for some of the best cuisine you'll find anywhere in Morocco.

Dar Moha €€€€€ *81 Rue Dar el-Bacha, Medina, tel: 024 38 64 00, <www.darmoha.ma>.* Open daily for lunch and Tues–Sun for dinner. The modern Moroccan cuisine served at Dar Moha is an amazing feast of flavours. Set in a beautiful villa that once belonged to French fashion designer Pierre Balmain.

Kechmara €€ *3 Rue de La Liberté, Guéliz, tel: 024 43 40 60.* Open daily for lunch and dinner. A popular place to be seen, offering good-value set menus with delicious and well-presented dishes. Great rooftop terrace and contemporary design. Better atmosphere at lunchtime than in the evening. Major credit cards.

Le Chat Qui Rit €€€ *92 Rue de Yougoslavie, Guéliz, tel: 024 43 43 11.* Open Tues eve to Saturday for lunch and dinner. Popular French/Italian restaurant owned by a Corsican. Pizzas, pasta, meat and fish dishes, reasonably priced and popular with local residents.

Le Foundouk €€€–€€€€ *55 Souk Hal Fassi Kat Bennahid, tel: 024 37 81 90, <www.foundouk.com>.* Open daily for lunch and dinner. One of Marrakech's most fashionable addresses, Foundouk serves a menu of French/international cuisine plus a long list of Moroccan favourites. The ambience is super-chic, and the restaurant offers indoor and outdoor dining.

Le Tobsil €€€€ *22 Derb Moulay Abdellah Ben Houceine, Baba Ksour, tel: 024 44 40 52.* One of a clutch of very high-quality traditional Moroccan restaurants, Tobsil offers refined dining in a beautifully restored *riad* in the medina. A popular restaurant, so booking is essential. Major credit cards.

MEKNES

Collier de La Colombe €€–€€€ *67 Rue Driba, Medina, tel: 035 55 50 41.* Open daily for lunch and dinner. Signs at the far end of Place Lalla Aouda direct you to this modern restaurant with sweeping views over the New Town. Fresh Atlas Mountain trout is a speciality. Several fixed-price Moroccan menus. Major credit cards.

Restaurant Riad €€€ *79 Ksar Chaacha-Dar Kebira, Medina, tel: 035 53 05 42.* Open daily for lunch and dinner. Below the ramparts of the medina, beyond Place Lalla Aouda, this is a gorgeous garden restaurant serving Moroccan specialities. Major credit cards.

RABAT

Dinarjat €€€–€€€€ *6 Rue Belgnaoui, near Avenue el-Alou, Medina, tel: 037 70 42 39.* Open daily for lunch and dinner. A beautiful, exotic setting for the best traditional Moroccan food in town. An attendant will lead you to the door, in the heart of the medina. Major credit cards.

Restaurant de la Plage €€€–€€€€ *Plage Oudaya, tel: 037 20 29 28.* Seafood restaurant overlooking the beach. Get a window seat and watch the sun set beyond the Atlantic surf. Major credit cards.

TANGIER

El Korsan €€€€ *Hotel El Minzah, 85 Rue de la Liberté, tel: 039 93 58 85.* Tangier's best and most lavish Moroccan restaurant will prepare *mechoui* (whole roasted lamb), if ordered at least a day in advance. Major credit cards.

Le Relais de Paris €€€ *Complexe Dawliz, tel: 039 33 18 19.* French brasserie in the Dawliz commercial centre overlooking the Straits of Gibraltar. The best French cuisine in town.

INDEX

Berlitz pocket guide

Morocco

14th Edition 2008
Reprinted 2010

Written by Neil Wilson
Updated by Charlie Shepherd
Series Editor: Tony Halliday

Photography credits
Alamy 28, 35, 51, 62, 93; istockphoto 64;
Chris Coe/Apa 3 (top middle), 12–13, 41, 81;
Tony Halliday 6, 71, 72, 76, 79, 82, 94, 102;
Clay Perry/Apa 8–9, 11, 19, 30, 56, 67, 68, 70,
75, 78, 85, 86, 89, 90, 91, 92, 95, 96, 99, 100,
103; Jean-Claude Vieillefond 33; Phil Wood/
Apa 14, 17, 20, 24, 37, 38, 40, 42, 44, 47, 48,
53, 54

Cover picture: Riccardo Spilla/4Corners

Printed in Singapore by Insight Print
Services (Pte) Ltd, 38 Joo Koon Road,
Singapore 628990. Tel: (65) 6865-1600.
Fax: (65) 6861-6438

Berlitz Trademark Reg. U.S. Patent Office
and other countries. Marca Registrada

Every effort has been made to provide
accurate information in this publication,
but changes are inevitable. The publisher
cannot be responsible for any resulting
loss, inconvenience or injury.

Contact us

At Berlitz we strive to keep our guides as
accurate and up to date as possible, but if you
find anything that has changed, or if you have
any suggestions on ways to improve this guide,
then we would be delighted to hear from you.

Berlitz Publishing, PO Box 7910,
London SE1 1WE, England.
fax: (44) 20 7403 0290
email: berlitz@apaguide.co.uk
www.berlitzpublishing.com